AF577276

Water: Rethinking Management in an Age of Scarcity

Sandra Postel

Worldwatch Paper 62
December 1984

Sections of this paper may be reproduced in magazines and newspapers with acknowledgment to Worldwatch Institute. The views expressed are those of the author and do not necessarily represent those of Worldwatch Institute and its directors, officers or staff.

©Copyright Worldwatch Institute, 1984
Library of Congress Catalog Card Number 84-52522
ISBN 0-916468-62-3

Printed on recycled paper

Table of Contents

Like energy, fresh water is essential to virtually every human endeavor. Its availability is vital to feeding the world's growing population, producing the material goods that raise living standards, and preserving the integrity of natural systems upon which life itself depends. The scarcity of anything so fundamental is bound to disrupt economic and social activity. Not surprisingly, after the sudden hardships wrought by oil price increases—the "energy crisis"—of the seventies, many people wonder if there might next be a crisis in water.

Numbers alone fail to tell water's true story. Enough rain and snow fall over the continents each year to fill Lake Huron 30 times, to magnify the flow of the Amazon sixteenfold, or to cover the earth's total land area to a depth of 83 centimeters. The volume of fresh water annually renewed by the water cycle could meet the material needs of 5 to 10 times the existing world population. Yet lack of water to grow crops periodically threatens millions with famine. Water tables in southern India, northern China, the Valley of Mexico, and the U.S. Southwest are falling precipitously, causing wells to go dry. Rivers that once ran year-round now fade with the end of the rainy season. Inland lakes and seas are shrinking.

I sincerely thank John Bredehoeft, Malin Falkenmark, Andrea Fella, Kenneth Frederick, John Harte, Jay Lear, Douglas Merrey, Helen Peters, and Peter Rogers for their helpful comments on early drafts of this manuscript, and Cynthia Pollock for her dedicated research assistance.

This paper will appear as the chapter "Managing Freshwater Supplies" in *State of the World 1985,* to be published by W.W. Norton & Co. in February 1985.

Always on the move, seemingly ubiquitous, and often hidden underground, water has long escaped the accounting books of many nations. Remarkably little is known with certainty about how much water is used where, when, and by whom. Although virtually every political leader could quote the current price of a barrel of oil, few would know the cost of securing an additional thousand cubic meters of water.

Unlike oil, metals, wheat, and most other vital commodities, water is usually needed in vast quantities that are too unwieldy to be traded internationally. Rarely is it transported more than several hundred kilometers from its source. Thus, while fresh water everywhere is linked to a vast global cycle, its value and adequacy as a resource is determined by the supplies available locally or regionally, and the way they are used and managed.

No historic event is likely to trigger a worldwide restructuring of water use the way the oil price hikes did for energy. Yet if current trends continue, fresh water may in many areas become a constraint on economic activity and food production over the coming decades. In the past, rivers and streams have been dammed and diverted to provide dependable water supplies to areas in need. Engineering feats, such as the Aswan Dam in Egypt and the California Aqueduct in the United States, have literally made deserts bloom. Yet increasing competition for limited supplies and the rising economic and environmental costs of traditional water strategies demand a new approach to the management of fresh water. Few governments have even recognized the need for such a reevaluation, much less begun to design the policies necessary for the future. Unfortunately, an abundance of time, as with an abundance of water, may very well prove illusory.

The Water Cycle and Renewable Supplies

Each year, the sun's energy lifts some 500,000 cubic kilometers of water from the earth's surface—86 percent from the oceans and 14 percent from land. (One cubic kilometer equals one billion cubic meters or one trillion liters; in standard U.S. usage, the equivalent is

"Remarkably little is known with certainty about how much water is used where, when, and by whom."

about 264 billion gallons.) An equal amount falls back to earth as rain, sleet, or snow, but fortunately not in the same proportions. Some 110,300 cubic kilometers falls over land (excluding Greenland and Antarctica), whereas only 71,500 is evaporated from it. Thus, this solar-powered cycle annually distills and transfers 38,800 cubic kilometers of water from the oceans to the continents. To complete the natural cycle, the water then makes its way back to the sea as "runoff."[1]

By virtue of this cyclic flow between the sea, air, and land, fresh water is a renewable resource. Under the planet's existing climatic conditions, approximately the same volume is made available each year. Today's supply is the same as when civilizations first dawned in the fertile river valleys of the Ganges, the Tigris-Euphrates, and the Nile. Viewed globally, fresh water is still undeniably abundant: For each human inhabitant there is now an annual renewable supply of 8,300 cubic meters, which is enough to fill a six-meter-square room 38 times, and several times the amount needed to sustain a moderate standard of living.[2]

Natural variations in climate and the vagaries of weather easily cast shadows over this picture of plenty, however, for water is not always available when and where it is most needed. Nearly two-thirds of each year's runoff flows rapidly away in floods, often bringing more destruction than benefit. The other third is stable, and is thus a reliable source of water for drinking or irrigating crops year-round. Water that infiltrates and flows underground provides the base flow of rivers and streams and accounts for most of the stable supply. The controlled release of water from lakes and reservoirs adds a bit more, bringing the total stable supply to about 14,000 cubic kilometers, or 3,000 cubic meters per person—the present practical limit of the renewable freshwater supply.

Asia and Africa are the continents facing the greatest water stress. Supplies for each Asian today are less than half the global average, and the continent's runoff is the least stable of all the major land masses. (See Table 1.) Lofty mountain ranges and a monsoon climate make rainfall and runoff highly variable. China's Huang He, or Yellow River, has had at least one major change of course every century

Table 1: Distribution of Renewable Freshwater Supplies, By Continent

Region	Average Annual Runoff	Share of Global Runoff	Share of Global Population	Share of Runoff That Is Stable
	(cubic kilometers)		(percent)	
Africa	4,225	11	11	45
Asia	9,865	26	58	30
Europe	2,129	5	10	43
North America[1]	5,960	15	8	40
South America	10,380	27	6	38
Oceania	1,965	5	1	25
Soviet Union	4,350	11	6	30
World	38,874	100	100	36[2]

[1]Includes Central America, with runoff of 545 cubic kilometers. [2]Average.

Sources: Adapted from M. I. L'vovich, *World Water Resources and Their Future,* translation edited by Raymond L. Nace (Washington, D.C.: American Geophysical Union, 1979); population figures are mid-1983 estimates from Population Reference Bureau, *1983 World Population Data Sheet* (Washington, D.C.: 1983).

of the 2,500 years of recorded Chinese history.[3] In India, 90 percent of the precipitation falls between the months of June and September, and most of the runoff flows in the Ganges and Brahmaputra basins in the North. Failure of the 1979 monsoon led to one of the worst droughts of recent record and reduced India's production of foodgrains by 16 percent.[4] In Africa, the Zaire River (formerly the Congo)—second in volume only to the Amazon—accounts for about 30 percent of the continent's renewable supplies but flows largely through sparsely populated rain forest. Two-thirds of the African nations have at least a third less annual runoff than the global average. Drought conditions that persistently plague the continent's dry regions have in recent years threatened over 20 nations with famine.[5]

North and South America and the Soviet Union all appear to have abundant water resources for their populations, though again great geographic disparities exist. South America appears the most richly endowed continent, yet 60 percent of its runoff flows in the channel of the Amazon, remote from most people and a hard source to tap. North and Central America together have a per capita water supply twice the global average, but natural supplies are limited in broad areas of the west, particularly in the southwestern United States and northern Mexico. The Soviet Union's three largest rivers—the Yenisei, the Lena, and the Ob'—all flow north through Siberia to the Arctic seas, far from the major population centers. Finally, Europe joins Asia as a continent with a substantially greater share of the world's people than of its fresh water. The continent's per capita runoff is only half the global average, and supplies are especially short in southern and eastern Europe. Fortunately, for much of the continent a generally temperate climate and a large number of smaller rivers with fairly steady flows allow a comparatively large share of the runoff to be tapped.

A detailed breakdown of supplies by country confirms water's unequal distribution. (See Table 2.) Per capita runoff ranges from over 100,000 cubic meters in Canada to less than 1,000 in Egypt. Yet even these national figures hide important disparities. On a per capita basis, Canada is the most water-wealthy nation in the world, but two-thirds of its river flow is northward, while 80 percent of its people live within 200 kilometers of the Canadian-U.S. border. Similarly, Indonesia appears to be a relatively water-rich nation, yet over 60 percent of the population lives on the island of Java, which has less than 10 percent of the country's runoff. Especially for the water-poor nations of Europe, Africa, and Asia, water flowing in from neighboring countries can be a vital addition to the runoff originating within their own borders. (The runoff estimates in Table 2 are consistent with a global water balance and thus include only runoff originating within each particular country.) Inflow accounts for roughly 70 percent of Czechoslovakia's water supplies, for example, roughly half of East and West Germany's, and 90 percent of Bulgaria's. Egypt, one of the most water-short nations in the world, is almost entirely dependent on the water of the Nile that enters the country from Sudan.[6]

Table 2: Average Annual Per Capita Runoff Produced in Selected Countries, 1983, With Projections for 2000

Country	1983	2000	Change
	(thousand cubic meters per person[1])		(percent)
Canada	110.0	95.1	−14
Norway	91.7	91.7	0
Brazil	43.2	30.2	−30
Venezuela	42.3	26.8	−37
Sweden	23.4	24.3	+4
Australia	21.8	18.5	−15
Soviet Union	16.0	14.1	−12
United States	10.0	8.8	−12
Indonesia	9.7	7.6	−22
Mexico	4.4	2.9	−34
France	4.3	4.1	−5
Japan	3.3	3.1	−6
Nigeria	3.1	1.8	−42
China	2.8	2.3	−18
India	2.1	1.6	−24
Kenya	2.0	1.0	−50
South Africa and Swaziland	1.9	1.2	−37
Poland	1.5	1.4	−7
West Germany	1.4	1.4	0
Bangladesh	1.3	0.9	−31
Egypt	0.09	0.06	−33
World	8.3	6.3	−24

[1]Estimates are for runoff originating within each specific country and do not include inflow from other countries.

Sources: M. I. L'vovich, *World Water Resources and Their Future*, translation edited by Raymond L. Nace (Washington, D.C.: American Geophysical Union, 1979); population figures are mid-1983 estimates from Population Reference Bureau, *1983 World Population Data Sheet* (Washington, D.C.: 1983).

"Population continues to grow fastest in some of the most water-short regions."

Given existing climatic conditions and current population projections, the per capita global water supply at the end of the century will have declined by 24 percent, while the stable, reliable component of that water will have dropped from 3,000 to 2,280 cubic meters per person. Population continues to grow fastest in some of the most water-short regions. Per capita supplies in Kenya and Nigeria, for example, will diminish by 50 and 42 percent, respectively. Supplies per person in Bangladesh and Egypt will diminish by a third, and in India by a fourth. Moreover, if projected climatic shifts from the rising concentration of atmospheric carbon dioxide materialize, water supplies may diminish in some areas already chronically water-short, including major grain-producing regions of north China and the United States.[7]

Competing Uses

When analysts speak of the "demand" for water, they typically refer to water's use as a commodity—as a factor of production in agriculture, industry, or household activities. Yet water in rivers, lakes, streams, and estuaries also is home to countless fish and plants, acts as a diluting and purifying agent, and offers a source of aesthetic enjoyment and richness that adds immeasurably to the quality of life. No society can draw on all its available supplies and hope to maintain the benefits water freely offers when left undisturbed. The need to protect these natural functions is thus a critical backdrop to considering society's pattern of water use.

Although the practice of irrigation dates back several thousand years to early Egyptian and Babylonian societies, and although water has been tapped to supply homes and small industries for centuries, for most of humanity's history water use expanded at a moderate pace. (Throughout this paper, the terms water use, withdrawal, and demand are used interchangeably; water consumption will be distinguished.) Over this century, however, demands have soared with rapid industrialization and the need to feed an expanding world population. According to estimates prepared by Soviet scientists in the early seventies for the U.N. International Hydrological Decade (1965-74), which are among the most comprehensive historical data available, world water use in 1900 was 400 billion cubic meters, or 242 cubic meters per person. By 1940 global usage had doubled, while population had increased about 40 percent. (See Figure 1.) A rapid rise in water demand then began at mid-century: By 1970 annual per capita withdrawals had climbed to over 700 cubic meters, 60 percent higher than in 1950. Both agricultural and industrial water use increased twice as much during these 20 years as they had over the entire first half of the century.[8]

Today, humanity's annual water withdrawals equal about a tenth of the total renewable supply and about a quarter of the stable supply—

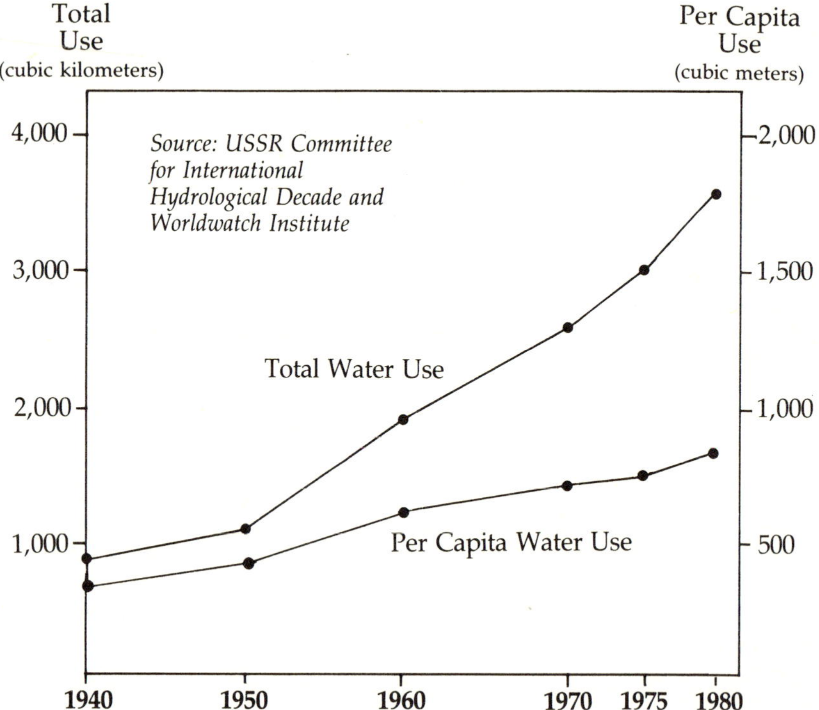

Figure 1: World Water Use, Total and Per Capita, 1940-80

"As fertile land became more scarce, irrigation enabled farmers to get higher yields from existing fields."

that which is typically available throughout a year. Agriculture claims the lion's share of world water use, accounting for about 70 percent of total withdrawals. As fertile land became more scarce, irrigation enabled farmers to get higher yields from existing fields, essentially substituting water for new cropland. With a controllable, year-round source of water, farmers also found it profitable to invest in fertilizer and to plant higher-yielding crop varieties. Yields of rain-fed rice, for example, typically increase by 50 percent if the effects of flood and drought can be eliminated, by 130 percent if controlled irrigation and drainage and some fertilizer are introduced, and by 280 percent or more if advanced irrigation techniques, generous fertilizer use, pest control, and high-yielding seeds are used.[9]

Roughly a third of today's harvest comes from the 17 percent of the world's cropland that is irrigated. Irrigation thus greatly helps meet the challenge of feeding an ever-growing population. Since 1950, the irrigated area worldwide has increased from 94 million to 261 million hectares. During the sixties, irrigation water was brought to an additional 6 million hectares each year; since 1970, an additional 5.2 million hectares have been added annually. (See Table 3.) At today's average rates of water use (some 11,000-12,000 cubic meters per irrigated hectare per year), and assuming irrigation continues to expand at a slightly diminishing rate, an additional 820 cubic kilometers of water will be needed for irrigation each year by the turn of the century—a 25-30 percent increase over existing levels.[10]

Besides demanding a large share of any region's available supplies, irrigation results in a large volume being "consumed"—removed from the local water supply through evaporation and transpiration. Crops must consume some water in order to grow, but typically much more water is transported and applied to fields than the crops require. Often less than half the water withdrawn for irrigation returns to a nearby stream or aquifer, where it can be used again. In the United States, for example, 55 percent of agricultural withdrawals are consumed, which in turn accounts for 81 percent of all the water consumed annually nationwide.[11]

Industry is the second major water-using sector of society, accounting for about a quarter of water use worldwide. Producing energy from

Table 3: Growth in Irrigated Area, By Continent, 1950-82

Region	Total Irrigated Area, 1982	Growth in Irrigated Area		
		1950-60	1960-70	1970-80[1]
	(million hectares)		(percent)	
Africa	12	25	80	33
Asia[2]	177	52	32	34
Europe[3]	28	50	67	40
North America	34	42	71	17
South America	8	67	20	33
Oceania	2	0	100	0
World	261	49	41	32

[1]Percentage increase between 1970 and 1982 prorated to 1970-80 to maintain comparison by decade. [2]Includes the Asian portion of the Soviet Union. [3]Includes the European portion of the Soviet Union.

Source: W.R. Rangeley, "Irrigation—Current Trends and a Future Perspective," prepared for World Bank Seminar, Washington, D.C., February 1983.

nuclear and fossil-fueled power plants is by far the largest single industrial water use. Water is the source of steam that drives the turbogenerators, and vast quantities are used to cool power plant condensers. Unlike in agriculture, however, only a small fraction of this water is consumed. Most existing power plants have "once-through" cooling systems that return water to its source immediately after it passes through the plant. U.S. plants, for example, consume only 2 percent of their withdrawals. Thus, especially when plants are situated next to large lakes or rivers, the volume of cooling water withdrawn is usually of less concern than the discharge of heated water back to the source. If lake or stream temperatures get too high, oxygen levels may drop, threatening fish and other aquatic life.[12]

Excluding energy production, two-thirds of the remaining industrial withdrawals go to just five industries: primary metals, chemical products, petroleum refining, pulp and paper manufacturing, and food processing. In countries with an established industrial base and water pollution laws in effect, withdrawals for these industries are not likely to increase. Most pollution control techniques involve recycling and reusing water, thus reducing an industry's demand for new supplies. Industrial use has declined, or is expected to decline soon, in countries such as Finland, Sweden, and the United States. In contrast, Portugal, the Soviet Union, Turkey, and several of the Eastern bloc nations are projecting a doubling of their industrial withdrawals over the century's last quarter. Increases of no more than 50 percent are expected in Czechoslovakia, France, and East and West Germany.[13]

Industry typically accounts for less than 10 percent of total withdrawals in most Third World countries, compared with 60-80 percent in most industrial nations. (See Table 4.) Much of the developing world is just embarking on the industrialization path taken by other countries four decades ago. Water demands for power production, manufacturing, mining, and materials processing are thus poised for a rapid increase if industries adopt the water-intensive technologies that those of the industrial world did. Industrial water use in Latin America, for example, is projected to jump 350 percent during the century's last quarter, compared with nearly 180 percent for drinking water and 70 percent for irrigation. (See Figure 2.) Among the targets set for the United Nations Second Development Decade is an 8 percent average annual rate of industrial growth for the Third World. Though this may prove too ambitious a goal, given the debt burden many of these countries face, the developing world's industrial water use could easily double by the end of the century.[14]

Water used by households—for drinking and cooking, bathing, washing clothes, and other activities—varies greatly with both income levels and the way in which water is supplied. In urban households with piped water available at the touch of a tap, daily use typically ranges between 100 and 350 liters per person. Households with water-intensive appliances, such as dishwashers and washing machines, and those where water is used to irrigate large lawns and gardens can use over 1,000 liters per person daily. In many developing countries, where water is supplied through a public hydrant, daily usage ranges between 20 and 70 liters per person. Areas such as Kenya, where women may walk several kilometers to draw water for their families, can record usages close to the biological minimum—2-5 liters per person daily.[15]

Table 4: Estimated Water Use in Selected Countries, Total, Per Capita, and by Sector, 1980

Country	Water Withdrawals: Total	Water Withdrawals: Per Capita	Share Withdrawn by Major Sectors: Agricultural	Share Withdrawn by Major Sectors: Industrial	Share Withdrawn by Major Sectors: Municipal[1]
	(billion liters per day)	(thousand liters per day)		(percent)	
United States	1,683	7.2	34	57	9
Canada	120	4.8	7	84	9
Soviet Union	967	3.6	64	30	6
Japan[2]	306	2.6	29	61	10
Mexico[2]	149	2.0	88	7	5
India[2]	1,058	1.5	92	2	6
United Kingdom	78	1.4	1	85	14
Poland	46	1.3	21	62	17
China	1,260	1.2	87	7	6
Indonesia[2]	115	0.7	86	3	11

[1]Along with residential use, figures may include commercial and public uses, such as watering parks and golf courses. [2]1975 figures for Mexico; 1977 for India, Indonesia, and Japan.

Sources: U.S. data, U.S. Geological Survey; Canadian data, Harold D. Foster and W.R. Derick Sewell, *Water: The Emerging Crisis in Canada* (Toronto: James Lorimer & Company, 1981); Soviet, U.K., Polish data, U.N. Economic Commission for Europe; Japanese, Indian, Indonesian data, *Global 2000 Report;* Mexican data, U.N. Economic Commission on Latin America; Chinese data, Vaclav Smil, *The Bad Earth.*

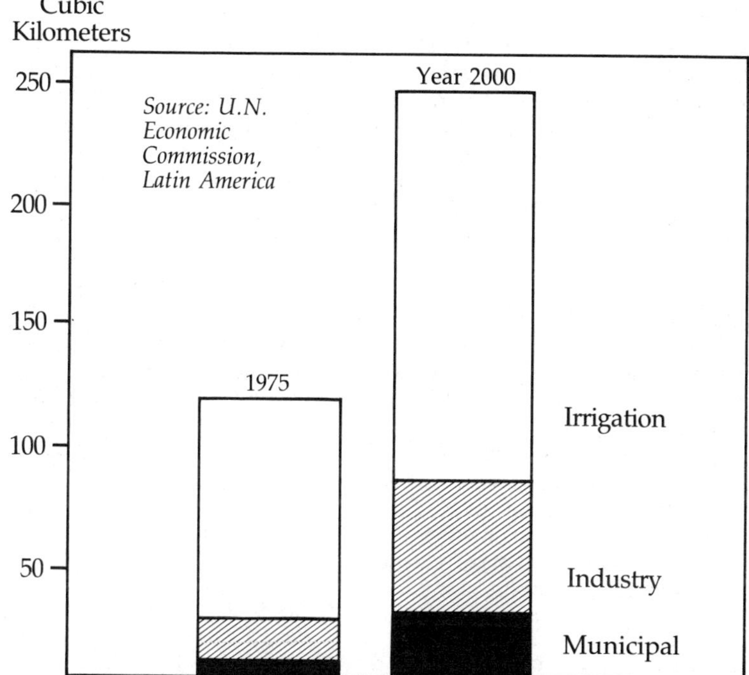

Figure 2: Annual Water Demands in Latin America, 1975, with Projections for 2000

Residential and other municipal uses of water account for less than a tenth of water withdrawals in many nations, and only about 7 percent of total withdrawals worldwide. In industrial countries where population growth is low and most households are already adequately supplied with water, growth in domestic demand is slowing and probably will continue to do so. In parts of Europe that are still converting from community wells to individual piped-water systems—including Czechoslovakia, Poland, Portugal, Romania, and

Turkey—demand for drinking water is expected to double over the next two decades. The largest increase will probably occur in the Third World, where freshwater supplies are not yet universally available. The World Health Organization estimates that as of 1980 only 75 percent of the developing world's urban dwellers and 29 percent of its rural population were served with drinking water. The United Nations has set a goal of providing safe water to all by 1990, which, although unlikely to be met, will contribute to a probable doubling of Third World domestic water demands by the end of the century.[16]

Even given these large increases in water withdrawals for irrigation, industrial, and domestic needs, total use worldwide by the year 2000 is still likely to be less than half the stable renewable supply. Yet projections by leading hydrologists show that meeting demands in North Africa and the Middle East will require virtually all the usable freshwater supplies in these regions. Usage in southern and eastern Europe, as well as central and southern Asia, will also be uncomfortably close to the volume of supplies these regions can safely and reliably tap.[17] Moreover, even if supplies appear more than adequate, no region is immune from the consequences of mismanagement and abuse that are already arising and that are bound to worsen as competing demands escalate.

The Consequences of Mismanagement

When a resource begins to show physical signs of abuse, economic and ecological consequences are usually not far behind. Water's seeming ubiquity has blinded society to the need to manage it sustainably and to adapt to the limits of a fixed supply. Mounting pressures are currently manifest in pervasive pollution, depletion of groundwater supplies, falling water tables, and damage to ecological systems. Failure to heed these signs of stress, and to place water use on a sustainable footing, threatens the viability of both the resource base itself and the economic systems that depend on it.

Each liter of polluted water discharged untreated contaminates many additional liters of fresh water in the receiving stream. The disposal of synthetic chemicals and heavy metals, which pose dangers in ex-

"As much as a fourth of the world's reliable water supply could be rendered unsafe for use by the year 2000."

tremely low concentrations, is an especially grave threat to the quality of water supplies. Without adequate treatment, the growing volume and toxicity of wastes could render as much as a fourth of the world's reliable supply unsafe for use by the year 2000.[18]

Many industrial countries now require that wastewaters meet specified standards of quality before they are discharged. Yet in most Third World countries, pollution controls are either nonexistent or unable to keep pace with urbanization and industrialization. In China, for example, only about 2 percent of the 28 billion cubic meters of wastewater discharged each year is treated. Already, a third of the water in its major rivers is polluted beyond safe health levels, and fish and shrimp have disappeared from 5 percent. China's first large wastewater treatment plant began operating in Beijing in the fall of 1980, but the volume of sewage far outpaces the facility's capacity to treat it. Wastewater flows in Beijing have increased twenty-sevenfold over the last three decades, and volumes for the country as a whole are projected to triple or quadruple by the end of the century.[19] Vaclav Smil, a specialist on China's environment, writes that the country's water pollution problem "will require very heavy and sustained investment—not to achieve zero discharges but merely to bring the appalling situation within reasonable limits after decades of no control."[20]

In virtually all of Latin America, municipal sewage and industrial effluents are discharged into the nearest rivers and streams without treatment. The pulp and paper and the iron and steel industries—two of the region's biggest polluters—have been growing twice as fast as the economy as a whole. Yet cleanup efforts have typically been postponed because of their high cost. Purifying Colombia's Bogota River, for example—one of the continent's most contaminated waterways—would cost an estimated $1.4 billion, a high price for a debt-ridden country to pay. Unless governments begin attacking urban and industrial pollution soon, however, they will inevitably face the prospect of a water supply too polluted for their people to drink.[21]

A similar situation exists in the Soviet Union. Industrial wastewaters comprise 10 percent of the Volga River's average flow at Volgograd, and three-fourths of the wastes are untreated. A major effort was begun in the mid-seventies to cleanse the river, but apparently enforcement has been too slack to encourage industries to install the costly technologies. Under these conditions, the Volga simply cannot sustain the existing high level of withdrawals and also remain of acceptable quality. According to Thane Gustafson, a U.S. specialist on Soviet affairs: "Footdragging by industry on pollution control will make it necessary to use more water for dilution. All these effects add up to a greater demand for water by the end of the century than the available supplies can satisfy."[22]

Vast quantities of the earth's water move slowly underground through the pores and fractures of geologic formations called aquifers. Some hold water thousands of years old and receive little annual replenishment from rainfall. Like oil reserves, water in these "fossil aquifers" is essentially nonrenewable; if tapped, it will in time be depleted. Even where recharge does occur, groundwater is often pumped at rates that exceed replenishment, causing water tables to fall and depleting future water reserves. Such overpumping—which geologists call water "mining"—supports only a fragile and short-term prosperity at best, for eventually the water becomes too salty to use, too expensive to pump to the surface, or runs out altogether.

One-fifth of the irrigated cropland in the United States is supported by water mined from a vast underground reserve called the Ogallala Aquifer. Stretching from southern South Dakota to northwest Texas, the aquifer underlies portions of eight states and spans an area roughly three times as big as the state of New York. Natural recharge is minimal in this semiarid region, and farmers have profitably irrigated corn, sorghum, and cotton only by drawing on water stored for thousands of years. Irrigation with Ogallala water began to expand rapidly in Texas in the forties, and when powerful pumping and irrigation systems were introduced it spread northward into Oklahoma, Kansas, and Nebraska during subsequent decades.[23] By 1978, over eight million hectares were under irrigation, compared with just 2.1 million in 1944. Over the last four decades, 500 cubic kilometers of groundwater have been withdrawn. Hydrologists estimate that the aquifer is now half depleted under 900,000 hectares of Kansas, New Mexico, and Texas.[24]

Faced with rising pumping costs, diminishing well yields, and low commodity prices, farmers are taking land out of irrigation. After several decades of steady growth, the total irrigated area in the High Plains is now declining. (See Figure 3.) In just four years, 1978 to 1982, irrigated land in Texas dropped by 20 percent, in Oklahoma by 18 percent, and in New Mexico by 9 percent. Collectively, in these and the other three states that draw most heavily on the Ogallala

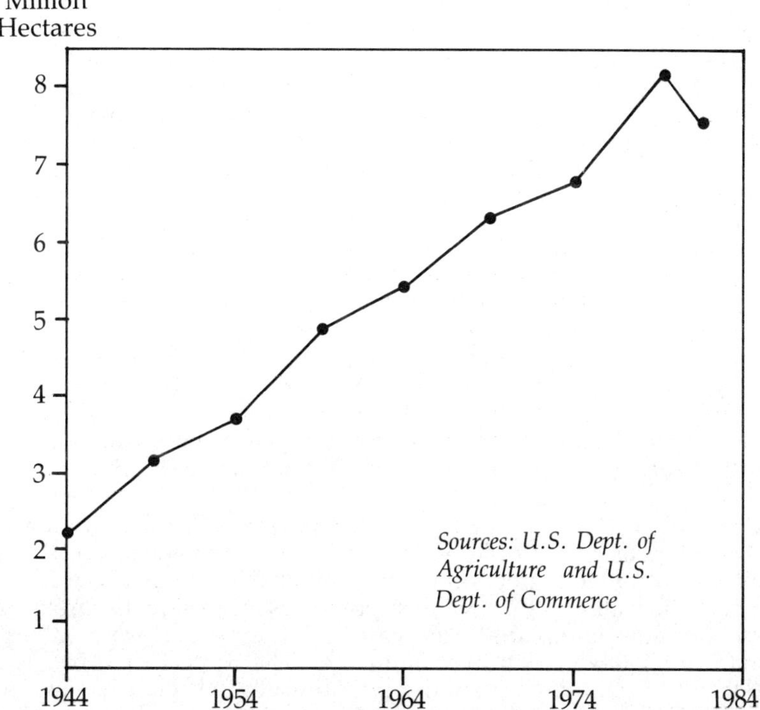

Figure 3: Irrigation Area in Six States That Rely Heavily on the Ogallala Aquifer, 1944-82

(Colorado, Kansas, and Nebraska), the total area under irrigation declined by 592,000 hectares, or 7 percent. In Nebraska, where a smaller portion of the Ogallala has been depleted, irrigation is still expanding. Yet in 1982, net returns from Northern Plains production of corn—the dominant irrigated crop in Nebraska—were less than half the national average, and it appears that eventually farmers there will begin switching crops, converting to dryland farming, or leaving agriculture altogether.[25]

Economists and government leaders are concerned about the potential collapse of a lucrative regional farming economy. The U.S. Army Corps of Engineers has even looked at the feasibility of massive river diversions to supply water to farmers now dependent on the diminishing Ogallala. But few have asked the more fundamental question of whether it makes sense to deplete this resource at a time when the nation can afford to preserve it. The U.S. Government is paying farmers to idle rain-fed cropland in order to lessen a price-depressing surplus of crops; at the same time, it is allowing the wholesale exhaustion of a unique water reserve to grow those same crops. Moreover, among the consequences predicted for much of the central and western United States from the rising level of atmospheric carbon dioxide is a reduction in the renewable water supply and an increase in the frequency and severity of droughts.[26] By exploiting the Ogallala today, farmers are foreclosing options to draw on it in the future when it may really be needed to meet vital food needs domestically and abroad. Failure to preserve this resource is shortsighted, and an error future generations will rightfully find hard to forgive.

Many other U.S. aquifers are suffering from overuse. Among the severest cases is one underlying Tucson, Arizona—the largest American city completely dependent on groundwater. Only about 35 percent of the water withdrawn to supply Tucson's residents, farms, and copper mines is replaced each year by recharge, and water tables in some areas have fallen over 50 meters. The Santa Cruz River is no longer sufficiently fed by underground water to keep it flowing during dry spells. Water levels have also dropped precipitously around El Paso in Texas and Ciudad Juarez in Mexico from the mining of the aquifer they share. In portions of the Dallas–Fort Worth metropolitan

> "Overpumping is epidemic in China's northern provinces."

area, water tables have fallen more than 120 meters over the last 25 years.[27]

Though rarely as well-documented as cases in the United States, excessive groundwater pumping and subsequent lowering of the water table appears to be increasingly common worldwide. (See Table 5.) Over the seventies, water levels dropped 25-30 meters in areas of Tamil Nadu in southern India, a consequence of uncontrolled pumping for irrigation. Overpumping is epidemic in China's northern provinces, where some 10 major cities rely heavily on groundwater for their basic supply. In Beijing, annual groundwater withdrawals exceed the sustainable supply by 25 percent, and water tables in some parts of the city have been dropping over 1 meter each year. In one district of Tianjin, a major manufacturing and commercial city, water tables are falling an astonishing 4.4 meters annually.[28]

Large withdrawals of groundwater may have other costly effects besides the depletion of future supplies. If water pumped from an aquifer susceptible to compaction is not replaced by recharge, the aquifer may compress, resulting in subsidence of the overlying land. Subsidence in Mexico City has damaged buildings and streets and disrupted the sewage system. In China, portions of Beijing have been sinking 20-30 centimeters annually since 1950, and rates of 10 centimeters per year have been measured in Tianjin. In the Houston-Galveston area of Texas, where water levels have declined 60 meters during the last half-century, portions of the land surface have sunk over 2 meters. High tides in the Gulf have flooded residential developments that, because of subsidence, are now closer to sea level.[29]

In coastal areas, heavy pumping may alter the volume and flow of groundwater discharging to the ocean and thereby allow sea water to invade the aquifer. Saltwater intrusion threatens to contaminate the drinking water supplies of many cities and towns along the U.S. Atlantic and Gulf coasts; it is especially severe in several Florida cities where pumping has pulled the water table below sea level. Israel, Syria, and the Arabian Gulf states are also battling threats of saltwater intrusion. Once it occurs, such contamination is difficult, if not impossible, to reverse.[30]

Table 5: Selected Cases of Excessive Water Withdrawals

Region	Status
Colorado River Basin, United States	Yearly consumption exceeds renewable supply by 5 percent, creating a water deficit; Colorado River is increasingly salty; water tables have fallen precipitously in areas of Phoenix and Tucson.
High Plains, United States	The Ogallala, a fossil aquifer that supplies most of the region's irrigation water, is diminishing; over a large area of the southern plains, the aquifer is already half depleted.
Northern China	Groundwater overdrafts are epidemic in northern provinces; annual pumping in Beijing exceeds the sustainable supply by 25 percent; water tables in some areas are dropping up to 1-4 meters per year.
Tamil Nadu, India	Heavy pumping for irrigation has caused drops in water table of 25-30 meters in a decade.
Israel, Arabian Gulf, and coastal United States	Intrusion of sea water from heavy pumping of coastal aquifers threatens to contaminate drinking water supplies with salt.
Mexico City; Beijing, China; Central Valley, California; Houston-Galveston, Texas	Groundwater pumping has caused compaction of aquifers and subsidence of land surface, damaging buildings, streets, pipes, and wells; hundreds of homes in a waterfront Texas community have been flooded.

California, United States	Water from Owens Valley and Mono Basin have been diverted to supply southern water users; Owens Lake has dried up, and Mono Lake's surface area has shrunk by a third.
Southwestern Soviet Union	Large river withdrawals have reduced inflow to the Caspian and Aral seas; the Caspian sturgeon fishery is threatened; the Aral's fisheries are virtually gone and the sea's volume may be halved by the turn of the century.

Source: Worldwatch Institute, based on various sources.

Excessive demands also take a toll on lakes, estuaries, and inland seas that are sustained by freshwater inflow from nearby rivers and streams. The Aral Sea in the southern Soviet Union is shrinking because of large withdrawals from its two major tributaries, the Amu Darya and Syr Darya. These two rivers help support Soviet Central Asia's lucrative agricultural economy, which includes more than half the nation's irrigated cropland. The population of several Central Asian republics has grown by 30 percent over the last decade, adding to pressures on the available water supply and to the importance of maintaining a thriving economy to secure more jobs in the region.[31] The Aral's level had remained fairly stable between 1900 and 1960, but has since dropped 9 meters. Fisheries that once figured prominently in the regional economy have virtually disappeared. Although officials are taking some measures to save portions of the Aral, they appear resigned to it shrinking further. Some scientists have projected that before the end of the century the sea may drop another 8-10 meters and its volume may be reduced by half.[32]

A similar scenario threatens to unfold further west in the Caspian Sea. The Volga River is the Caspian's main source of inflow, helping to replenish the large quantities of water evaporated from the sea each year. Construction of large dams on the river during the fifties and subsequent irrigation withdrawals dramatically reduced the river's discharge into the Caspian. The sea reached its lowest level in centuries in 1977, having dropped more than 3 meters over the preceding half-century. The level has risen somewhat in recent years because of unusually heavy rains that increased the Volga's flow. But Soviet scientists do not expect this fortuitous occurrence to continue. According to U.S. geographer Philip Micklin, who discussed the situation during a five-month stay in the Soviet Union in 1984, additional diversions for irrigation are planned for the Volga, and the Caspian's level is expected to drop further over the next decade. The sea supports bountiful fisheries, including 90 percent of the world's catch of sturgeon. Salmon and migratory herring spawn in the Volga and feed in the North Caspian. Substantial damage to these fisheries is likely to occur if the sea's level declines much further.[33]

Shrinking inland seas are a dramatic consequence of large water withdrawals to meet irrigation and other water demands. But an equally grave threat is the quiet loss of fish and other aquatic life from rivers and streams whose altered flow patterns can no longer sustain them. As long as water withdrawals remain well below a region's average sustainable supply, streamflows will be sufficient to safeguard most ecological values. Yet where a large share of surface water is diverted from its natural channels, these benefits may be lost.

Over the last decade, many nations have begun to realize this danger, but they are not prepared to avert it. Setting minimum flow levels to protect wildlife requires large quantities of data and the expertise of hydrologists, fisheries biologists, and aquatic ecologists. The quick and inexpensive methodologies are simply not accurate enough to be reliable. A common one, for example, sets minimum flow requirements as a fixed percentage (such as 10 percent) of the average annual flow. But this makes no allowance for the large flow variability that typifies many river basins, nor for the long-term, cumulative effects on fish of low flows for extended periods of time. More sophisticated methods usually involve a computer model that quantifies, for each particular species, the amount of habitat available in a given stretch of the stream at each stage of its life cycle and under varying streamflow conditions. Though more accurate, such methods are time-

"**Waterlogging and salinization are sterilizing some 1 million to 1.5 million hectares of fertile soil annually.**"

consuming and costly, requiring much field data and scientific expertise to interpret them.[34] A paper issued in 1984 by the Canadian Inquiry on Federal Water Policy acknowledges that "in Canada, we are only beginning to appreciate the magnitude of water needs for the support of the ecosystem. We do not have very reliable estimates of instream requirements."[35]

Among the least affordable consequences of irrational water use is the degradation of valuable cropland from poor irrigation practices. Irrigation water is typically brought to crops through unlined canals and ditches that allow vast quantities of water to seep down to the water table. Where drainage is inadequate, the water level gradually rises, eventually entering the crops' root zone and waterlogging the soil. In the Indian state of Madhya Pradesh, for example, a large irrigation project that originally was expected to increase crop production tenfold led to extensive waterlogging and, consequently, a reduction in corn and wheat yields. Farmers there now refer to their once fertile fields as "wet deserts."[36]

In dry climates, waterlogging may be accompanied by salinization as water near the surface evaporates and leaves behind a damaging residue of salt. According to some estimates, waterlogging and salinization are sterilizing some 1 million to 1.5 million hectares of fertile soil annually. The problem is especially severe in India and Pakistan (where an estimated 12 million hectares have been degraded), the Valley of Mexico, the Helmud Valley in Afghanistan, the Tigris and Euphrates basins in Syria and Iraq, the San Joaquin Valley in California, the North Plain of China, and Soviet Central Asia.[37] In these areas, waterlogging and/or salinization threaten to diminish the very gains in food production that costly new irrigation projects are intended to yield.

Augmenting Dependable Supplies

When natural water supplies become inadequate to meet a region's demands, water planners and engineers historically have responded by building dams to capture and store runoff that would otherwise flow through the water cycle "unused" and by diverting rivers to redistribute water from areas of lesser to greater need. As the demand for water has increased, so have the number and scale of these engineering endeavors to augment available supplies. Tens of thousands of dams now span the world's rivers. Collectively, their reservoirs store roughly 2,000 cubic kilometers of runoff, increasing by 17 percent the 12,000 cubic kilometers of naturally stable runoff derived from groundwater and lakes. Most of this capacity has been added since mid-century, when the pace of large dam construction abruptly quickened. All but 7 of the 100 largest dams in the world were completed after World War II.[38]

Many industrial countries are now finding, however, that the list of possible dam sites is growing shorter and that the cost of adding new storage facilities is rising rapidly. In the United States, for example, reservoir capacity grew on average 80 percent per decade between the twenties and the sixties. As the narrow valley sites were gradually exploited, any new capacity required broader, earth-filled dams. By the sixties, 36 times more dam material was needed to create a given reservoir capacity than in the twenties. With a corresponding escalation in construction costs, reservoir development markedly declined.[39]

In most of Europe, a favorable climate and geography for securing water supplies has lessened the need to build large storage reservoirs, compared with, for example, the western United States. Yet to meet rising demands, many European nations plan large increases in reservoir capacity over the next decade. (See Table 6.) A 1981 report prepared by the U.N. Economic Commission for Europe (ECE) raises doubts, however, about the ambitious plans of several countries materializing. Both high costs and growing opposition to the flooding of farmlands and valleys are becoming major barriers to dam construction. Notwithstanding government forecasts that "optimistically predict" a doubling or tripling in reservoir capacity, the ECE assessment concludes that some countries have already reached the practical limits of their reservoir development.[40]

Lagging the industrial world's big dam era by two decades, dam construction in the developing world is now in its heyday. Two-thirds of the dams over 150 meters high slated for completion this decade

"By the sixties, 36 times more dam material was needed to create a given reservoir capacity than in the twenties."

Table 6: Reservoir Capacity in Selected Countries, 1970, With Projections to 1990

Country	Total Capacity	Projected Increase in Capacity, 1970-90
	(cubic kilometers)	(percent)
Belgium	0.1	79
Bulgaria	2.7	296
Canada	518.0	—
Czechoslovakia	3.3	76
East Germany	0.9	156
France	2.0	—
Greece	8.7	78
Poland	26.0	127
Portugal	5.3	119
Romania	2.6	746
Sweden	27.1	0
Soviet Union	830.0	60
United Kingdom	1.5	47
United States	670.0	15
West Germany	2.3	—

Source: United Nations Economic Commission for Europe, *Long-Term Perspectives for Water Use and Supply in the ECE Region* (New York: United Nations, 1981).

are in the Third World.[41] Designed mainly for generating hydroelectric power and supplying water for irrigation, large dams and reservoirs offer promises of greater energy independence and food self-sufficiency. Their lure is understandable as large-scale solutions to a set of large development dilemmas. Unfortunately, high costs, poor planning, and environmental disruption are leaving a legacy of failed expectations that suggest they are not the panacea once envisioned.

Sri Lanka's Mahaweli Development Programme encompasses construction of four large dams across the Mahaweli River to help achieve goals of tripling the nation's electric generating capacity and irrigating an additional 130,000 hectares of cropland. Yet with only two dams completed, the project's long-term viability already appears jeopardized. Capital costs nearly doubled in just four years, severely straining the government's finances. Inspections by agencies donating to the project—including the Agency for International Development and the World Bank—uncovered serious design and construction problems which in 1982 led to the conclusion that without major corrective efforts the irrigation canals would not function as planned. Studies had warned that unless deforested hillsides were replanted, runoff would wash large amounts of soil downstream, threatening a buildup of silt in reservoirs and irrigation canals and a lowering of soil fertility. Yet reforestation did not begin until more than a decade after initiation of the project, and by the end of 1982 replanting had taken place on less than 1 percent of the area targeted for it. Writer John Madeley notes, "The homes of 45,000 people are being flooded by the Victoria Dam, and, when they move into the new resettlement zone, their hopes of making a new living will not have been helped by the lack of attention to replanting."[42]

The experience Sri Lanka has had with the Mahaweli project is by no means unique. Though undertaken with good intentions of raising food production and living standards, large dam schemes are often so costly and complex that other critical tasks—often essential to the project's success—are neglected. As described earlier, vast areas of valuable cropland are becoming waterlogged and salt-laden because of excessive seepage from reservoirs and canals and poor drainage from fields. Deforestation and overgrazing are disrupting water's flow through the landscape. Natural forests and grasslands absorb runoff and allow it to move slowly through the subsurface. As hillsides are denuded, rainfall and soil run rapidly off in floods, filling expensive reservoirs with silt and causing dry-weather streamflows to disappear.

Especially in the Third World, managing watersheds to stabilize runoff is critical to reversing a vicious cycle of flooding, soil loss, declining crop production, and perennial drought. In Malaysia, conversion

"**Deforestation—now estimated at 11.3 million hectares per year—may be diminishing the Third World's stable runoff by as much as expensive new dams and reservoirs are augmenting it.**"

of natural forest to rubber and palm oil plantations has doubled peak runoff and cut dry-season flows in half. Deforestation on the small island of Dominica has contributed to a 50 percent reduction in dry-weather flows there.[43] Though virtually impossible to quantify, it may well be that deforestation—now estimated at 11.3 million hectares per year—is diminishing the Third World's stable runoff by as much as expensive new dams and reservoirs are augmenting it. Unless the threats posed by deforestation, waterlogging, and soil salinization are countered, large dam schemes may end up wasting capital and degrading land while bringing few lasting benefits to those they are intended to serve.[44]

As with dams and reservoirs, projects to divert water from one river basin to another have grown in number and scale in response to rising demand. Proposals to import water from some distant source have been made for virtually every major region facing a shortage. Most were developed during an era of cheap energy, relatively cheap capital, and when environmental values rarely entered the debate over project costs and benefits. The collective history of these large diversion schemes is marked by long study times, periodic abandonment, multibillion-dollar cost estimates, and growing concern over their ecological effects. (See Table 7.) Some of these projects will probably never leave the drawing boards. Those that do, and that are actually completed, may be more a product of political expediency than of an objective analysis of alternative ways to achieve a given end.

In China, officials and scientists began in the early fifties to study the possibility of diverting water from the Chang Jiang (Yangtze) river basin in central China to the water-poor regions of the north. After years of lying dormant, the project was given a boost in February 1983 when the government approved the first stage of work on what is known as the East Route.[45] This mainly involves reconstructing the old Grand Canal, which will offer navigation benefits regardless of whether other phases of the project are completed. The long-term plans call for pumping water 660 kilometers north to the Huang He, the Yellow River, from which it would flow an additional 490 kilometers by gravity into the vicinity of Tianjin. Chinese water planners estimate that the diversion will require several dozen pumping stations with a total installed capacity of about 1,000 megawatts—

Table 7: Selected Major River Diversion Projects

Project	Distance	Planned Annual Volume	Estimated Capital Cost	Current Status
	(kilometers)	(cubic kilometers)	(billion dollars)	
Chang Jiang River—North China Plain, China	1,150	15.0	5.2[1]	Decision in 1983 to begin construction
Northern European Rivers—Caspian Sea Basin, Soviet Union	3,500	20.0	3.1	Construction to begin in 1986
Siberian Rivers—Central Asia, Soviet Union	2,500	25.0	41.0	Preparing engineering designs; decision pending
Central Arizona Project, United States	536	1.5	3.5	Deliveries to Phoenix to begin Dec. 1985; to Tucson, 1991.
California State Water Project, United States	715	5.2	3.8[2]	Operating at 60 percent of planned capacity
Midwest Rivers—High Plains, United States[3]	600-1,600	2.0-7.4	5.5-35.0	No action

[1]A published estimate considered low by project analysts; cost could easily double. [2]Includes only costs incurred and projected through 1995; State has yet to develop new proposals (and cost estimates) to significantly increase the project's capacity over existing levels. [3]Five different diversions were studied. Lower figure of each range is for diversion of Missouri River into western Kansas, the least costly alternative; higher figure is for diversion of several south-central rivers into Oklahoma and Texas panhandles, the most costly alternative.

Source: Worldwatch Institute, based on various sources.

equal to one very large nuclear or coal plant. The system would transfer about 15 cubic kilometers of water in an average year, and up to double that volume in a dry year. Most of the water would be used to expand or improve irrigation on 4.3 million hectares; the remainder would enhance Tianjin's municipal and industrial water supply.[46]

With an estimated price tag of $5.2 billion, which analysts say could easily double, Chinese officials are understandably proceeding cautiously. Bruce Stone, one of a team of experts studying the Chinese diversion proposals, makes a convincing case that the water transfer may be an unnecessarily costly and risky way to raise grain production on the North China Plain. He notes that most of the irrigated cropland near Tianjin now yields only 1.8 tons per hectare, while a smaller portion yields 2.3 tons. The production increase gained by expanding irrigation to 1 average-yielding hectare could therefore be obtained equally by upgrading 3 or 4 hectares already under irrigation to produce the higher yields. Moreover, without better management and drainage of irrigated lands, the diverted water may worsen the salinization of North Plains' farmland. Salinization is already reducing yields on 2.7 million hectares, and another 4.7 million are threatened.[47]

Officials in the Soviet Union have in recent years revived century-old ideas of diverting north-flowing rivers to the more populous southern European and central Asian regions. One project aims to transfer water from northern European lakes and rivers to the Volga drainage basin, the primary purpose being to stabilize the level of the Caspian Sea. Even more ambitious is the proposed diversion of Siberian rivers south to the central Asian republics, where water deficits of 100 cubic kilometers are projected by the turn of the century. The region's burgeoning population and intensifying political clout have increased pressure to find some solution to its pending water shortage and unemployment problems. Thane Gustafson observed in 1980 that apparently "the latitude enjoyed by technical specialists to criticize or oppose the diversion projects has become hostage to the projects' political priority." The greatest single obstacle to proceeding with the diversions, he noted, was "the tightness of investment capital, which makes a full-scale commitment by the leadership unlikely in the near term."[48]

In January 1984, nevertheless, the USSR Council of Ministers called for a detailed engineering design for the entire 2,500-kilometer route from the Ob' River to the Amu Darya. Construction could begin by 1988 if the designs are accepted, and water that now drains into the Arctic may be heading to the cotton lands and industries of central Asia by the end of the century. Cost estimates for the initial transfer capacity of 25 cubic kilometers are $18 billion for the main diversion canal and $23 billion for the facilities to distribute the water once it reaches its destination.[49] Meanwhile, some Soviet scientists still maintain there is considerable potential to increase the efficiency of water use in the destination region. According to one estimate, conservation in agriculture and industry could save up to half the initial volume of the proposed transfer. Moreover, as with China's project, the diverted water could spread the already severe salinization of irrigated land.[50]

In the United States, no new federal water projects have been authorized since 1976, though since the turn of the century authorization bills have been introduced into the U.S. Congress about every two years. More importantly, actual funding for water project construction (excluding wastewater treatment) has declined steadily over the past eight years; appropriations in 1984 were about 70 percent less in

"Tight capital and $180-billion federal deficits are forcing to an end a long era of massive water subsidies."

real terms than in 1976.[51] Tight capital and $180-billion federal deficits are forcing to an end a long era of massive water subsidies. Historically, few of these projects have returned sufficient benefits to justify their high costs. An example is the Central Arizona Project (CAP), a large diversion of the Colorado River to supply the growing population in Arizona. Long before the first drops of CAP water were destined for Phoenix and Tucson, economist Thomas Power of the University of Montana stated that not only was the project's benefit-cost ratio less than one, "it may well only return a few cents of each dollar invested in it."[52]

Public opposition is adding another large hurdle to water project construction in the United States—in some cases, perhaps an insurmountable one. The California State Water Project (SWP) is a case in point. One of the most complex water schemes ever designed, SWP is now operating at 60 percent of its planned annual capacity. Capital costs to date total about $3.4 billion, and the need to lift much of the water 590 meters over the Tehachapi Mountains guarantees high energy bills: Pumping costs in 1983 totaled over $100 million.[53]

Two successive state administrations in California have failed to win sufficient support for additional SWP facilities that would allow more northern water to be transferred to Los Angeles and the agricultural valleys in the south. The voters rejected one proposal, called the Peripheral Canal, in a 1982 referendum. This defeat reflected concern about the canal's ecological effects around the Sacramento-San Joaquin Delta and, more fundamentally, about the merits of costly water exports versus stronger conservation efforts by southern water users. Another proposal, known as the "through-delta" plan, died in the California assembly in August 1984 when it appeared to proponents that another public referendum could not be avoided. Approval of any plan within the next few years that would substantially increase the volume of water shipped south appears increasingly doubtful.[54]

As the prospects for dams and diversions to augment dependable water supplies become less promising, the potential to store surplus runoff underground is receiving more attention. Artificially recharging underground aquifers—either by spreading water over land that allows it to percolate downward or by injecting it through a well—is one way to both stabilize water tables and increase the amount of runoff stored for later use. Underground storage also avoids damming a free-flowing river, minimizes competition for valuable land, and prevents large losses of water through evaporation, which are among the principal objections to surface reservoirs.

More than 20 countries now have active projects to artificially recharge groundwater. Yet in just a few cases has the practice been adopted on a large scale. Israel transports 300 million cubic meters of water from north to south every year through its National Water Carrier System and stores two-thirds of it underground. The water is used to meet high summer demands and offers a reliable source of supply during dry years.[55] In the United States, local water agencies in California, which have been recharging groundwater since the twenties, now place nearly 2.5 billion cubic meters in underground basins each year. The state's Department of Water Resources also began to seriously investigate groundwater storage as the options for damming more surface streams became increasingly limited. By 1980, the department had 34.5 million cubic meters stored in two separate State Water Project demonstration areas. Preliminary estimates for seven groundwater basins indicate a potential for augmenting the SWP's annual yield by about 500 million cubic meters, at unit costs at least 35-40 percent lower than the median cost of water from new surface reservoirs.[56] Also, the U.S. Congress enacted legislation in the fall of 1984 authorizing demonstration projects in 17 western states to recharge aquifers, including the diminishing Ogallala.[57]

Underground storage may hold special potential for Third World countries subjected to the destructive flooding and perennial dry spells of a monsoon climate. Capturing excessive runoff and storing it underground can convert damaging flood waters into a stable source of supply, while avoiding the large evaporation losses that occur with surface reservoirs. In India, subsurface storage has sparked interest as a way of providing a reliable source of irrigation water for the productive soils of the Gangetic Plain. According to some estimates, a fully irrigated Plain could grow crops sufficient for three-fourths of India's population.[58] On the North Plain of China, also prone to chronic drought, water from nearby surface streams is diverted into

"Capturing excessive runoff and storing it underground can convert damaging flood waters into a stable source of supply."

an underground storage area with a capacity of 480 million cubic meters. When fully recharged, the aquifer will supply irrigation water for 30,000 hectares of farmland. Several counties in Hebei Province are also artificially recharging aquifers to combat sinking water tables.[59]

Many aquifers are also recharged unintentionally by seepage from irrigation canals. In such cases, managing groundwater in conjunction with the surface irrigation water can help prevent waterlogging and salinization and may allow for an expansion of irrigated area without developing additional surface water sources. Such a strategy has been tried in the Indus Valley of Pakistan where a 60,000-kilometer network of canals sits atop a vast groundwater reservoir. By the mid-sixties, leakage from the canals had tripled the volume of recharge to the aquifer, and the resulting rise in the water table caused extensive waterlogging. Following a World Bank-sponsored study of the area, the Pakistan Government began to subsidize the installation of tubewells to tap the vast amount of water that had collected underground over the decades. About 11,000 public wells have been installed under the government program, and individual farmers have constructed over 100,000 private wells, which, though built to supply them with irrigation water, also help control waterlogging. Unfortunately, much of the water pumped is too saline for use unless mixed with purer surface water, and poor operation and maintenance have apparently made the public wells a burden to the government. Yet the strategy of jointly managing groundwater and surface water may offer substantial benefits where the physical setting is right and the needed technical and institutional coordination can be developed.[60]

Artificial recharge on a small scale has helped augment local water supplies for decades. The North Dakota town of Minot, for example, opted for this approach when faced with chronic water shortages and rapidly declining groundwater levels. Its complete recharge system cost only 1 percent as much as building a pipeline to the Missouri River, another of the town's supply alternatives. After six months of operation, water levels in portions of the aquifer had risen more than six meters.[61] Despite a host of similar local-level success stories, however, the practice is far from realizing its potential. According to Jay

H. Lehr, Executive Director of the National Water Well Association in the United States, the efficiency of storing surplus runoff underground "has been proven the world over. The costs, while by no means negligible, are reasonable in the face of other sound alternatives and a steal when compared to the grandiose water schemes of the mega minds of the Army Corps of Engineers and the Bureau of Reclamation."[62] Soviet scientist M.I. L'vovich has predicted that "the 21st century will undoubtedly be the century of underground reservoirs."[63]

Of the less conventional ways to augment a region's freshwater supplies—such as seeding clouds to induce precipitation, towing icebergs, and desalting sea water—desalination appears to hold the greatest near-term potential. Indeed, with the oceans holding 97 percent of all the water on earth, desalted sea water seems to offer the ultimate solution to a limited renewable freshwater supply. Several technologies have proved effective, but their large energy requirements make them too expensive for widespread use. Desalting sea water is typically 10 times more costly than supplying water from conventional sources, and applying the process to brackish (slightly salty) water is 2.5 times more costly. Total desalination capacity worldwide is now 2.7 cubic kilometers per year, less than one-tenth of 1 percent of global water use. Sixty percent of the world's capacity is in the Arabian Peninsula and Iran, where surface water is virtually nonexistent and even groundwater is often too salty to drink. Yet even in these energy-rich countries, producing and transporting the desalted water inland is in some cases prohibitively expensive. Though perhaps the ultimate source, desalination is unlikely to deliver its promise of a limitless supply of fresh water any time soon.[64]

Conserving Water

As affordable options to augment dependable water supplies diminish, the key to feeding the world's growing population, sustaining economic progress, and improving living standards will be learning to use existing supplies more efficiently. Using less water to grow grain, make steel, and flush toilets increases the water available

"Raising irrigation efficiencies worldwide by just 10 percent would save enough water to supply all global residential water uses."

for other uses as surely as building a dam or diverting a river does. The outlines of a strategy to curb water demand are clear, though no single blueprint can apply to every region. The challenge is to combine the technologies, economic policies, laws, and institutions that work best in each water setting.

Since agriculture claims the bulk of most nations' water budgets and is by far the largest consumer, saving even a small fraction of this water frees a large amount to meet other needs. Raising irrigation efficiencies worldwide by just 10 percent, for example, would save enough water to supply all global residential water uses. As discussed previously, vast quantities of water seep through unlined canals while in transit to the field, and much more water is applied to crops than is necessary for them to grow. The rising cost of new irrigation projects, the limited supplies available to expand watering in many areas, and the high cost of pumping are forcing governments, international lending agencies, and farmers alike to find ways of making agricultural water use more efficient.

Most farmers in developing as well as industrial countries use gravity-flow systems to irrigate their fields. The oldest method, and generally the least expensive to install, these systems distribute water from a groundwater well or surface canal through unlined field ditches or siphons. Typically, only a small portion reaches the crop's root zone; a large share runs off the field. Sprinkler systems, which come in many varieties, apply water to the field in a spray. They use more energy than gravity systems and require a larger capital investment to install, but they have brought irrigation to rolling and steep lands otherwise suited only for dryland farming. One design—the center pivot system—was largely responsible for the rapid expansion of irrigation on the U.S. High Plains in recent decades.[65]

Drip or trickle irrigation systems, developed in Israel in the sixties, supply water and fertilizer directly onto or below the soil. An extensive network of perforated piping releases water close to the plants' roots, minimizing evaporation and seepage losses. These costly systems thus far have been used mainly for high-value orchard crops in water-short areas. Today drip irrigation is used on about 10 percent of Israel's irrigated land, where experiments in the Negev Desert have shown per-hectare yield increases of 80 percent over sprinkler systems. Introduced into the United States in the early seventies, these systems now water nearly 200,000 hectares and are slowly being used on row crops too.[66] In Brazil's drought-plagued northeast, a project sponsored by the Inter-American Development Bank is experimenting with one design to irrigate crops where farm incomes are low and water supplies are scarce.[67]

Most irrigation experts agree that the actual efficiency of water use obtained in the field depends as much on the way the irrigation system is managed as on the type used. Although drip irrigation may be inherently more efficient by design, the wide average range of efficiency for each system—40-80 percent for gravity flow, 75-85 percent for a center pivot sprinkler, and 60-92 percent for a drip system—shows that management is a key determinant. Farmers using conventional gravity-flow systems, for example, can cut their water demands by 30 percent by capturing and recycling the water that would otherwise run off the field. Some U.S. jurisdictions now require these tailwater reuse systems. Farmers are also finding, however, that they often make good economic sense because pumping tailwaters back to the main irrigation ditch generally requires less energy than pumping new water from the source, especially from a deep well.[68]

Farmers can also reduce water withdrawals by scheduling their irrigation according to actual weather conditions, evapotranspiration rates, soil moisture, and their crops' water requirements. Although this may seem like fine tuning, careful scheduling can cut water needs by 20-30 percent. At the University of Nebraska's Institute of Agriculture and Natural Resources, a computer program called "IRRIGATE" uses data gathered from small weather stations across the state to calculate evapotranspiration from the different crops grown in each area. Farmers can call a telephone hotline to find out the amount of water used by their crops the preceding week, and then adjust their scheduled irrigation date accordingly. The California Department of Water Resources is launching a similar management system with a goal of saving 740 million cubic meters of water annually by the year 2010. The Department is also demonstrating irrigation management techniques through mobile laboratories equipped to evaluate the efficiencies of all types of irrigation systems—gravity, sprinkler, and drip—and to recommend ways that farmers can use their water more efficiently.[69]

Israel has pioneered the development of automated irrigation, in which the timing and amount of water applied is controlled by computers. The computer not only sets the water flow, it also detects leaks, adjusts water application for wind speed and soil moisture, and optimizes fertilizer use. The systems typically pay for themselves within three to five years through water and energy savings and higher crop yields. Motorola Israel Ltd., the main local marketer of automated systems, has begun exporting its product to other countries; by 1982 over 100 units had been sold in the United States. Israel's overall gains in agricultural water use efficiency, through widespread adoption of sprinkler and drip systems and optimum management practices, have been impressive: The average volume of water applied per hectare declined by nearly 20 percent between 1967 and 1981, allowing the nation's irrigated area to expand by 39 percent while irrigation water withdrawals rose by only 13 percent.[70]

In the Third World, where capital for construction of new projects is increasingly scarce, better management of existing irrigation systems may be the best near-term prospect for increasing crop production and conserving water supplies. Lining irrigation canals, for example, can help reduce water waste, prevent waterlogging, and eliminate the erosion and weed growth that makes irrigation ditches deteriorate.[71] Yet canal lining is expensive, and other options may prove more cost-effective. Seepage from canals is not necessarily water wasted since it increases the potential groundwater supply. By coordinating the use and management of groundwater and surface water, as in the case of the Indus Valley described earlier, the total efficiency of water use in an agricultural region can be increased.

Farmers also need control of their irrigation water in order to make good use of fertilizer and other inputs that increase crop yields. Concrete turnouts that allow farmers to better dictate the timing and flow of water to their fields, for example, are being built in India, Pakistan, and elsewhere.[72] At a pilot project in Egypt, funded by the U.S. Agency for International Development, improved management of irrigation systems is largely credited with boosting rice yields 35 percent. Water savings alone will often justify such investments: By some estimates, better irrigation management in Pakistan could annually save over 50 cubic kilometers—four times the storage capacity of the nation's Tarbela Dam—at one-fourth the cost of developing new water supplies.[73]

Curbing industrial demand for water, the second major draw on world supplies, tackles problems in two ways: It frees a large volume of fresh water to meet other competing demands, and it can greatly reduce the volume of polluted water discharged to local rivers and streams. In most developing countries, industry's demand for water is growing faster than that of either agriculture or municipalities. A slowdown is thus essential for sustained economic growth in water-short regions and for battling pollution problems that are fast making available supplies unfit for use.

In many industries, much of the water used is for cooling and other processes that do not require that it be of drinking-water quality. A large share of the water initially withdrawn can thus be recycled several times before disposing of it. Thermal power plants can cut their requirements by 98 percent or more by using recycled water in cooling towers rather than the typical once-through cooling methods. Palo Verde, a nuclear power plant built in the desert outside Phoenix, Arizona, for example, is near no body of water; it will draw on nearby communities' treated wastewater, which the plant will reuse 15 times.[74] The water needs of other industries also vary greatly, depending on the degree of recycling: Manufacturing a ton of steel may take as much as 200,000 liters or as little as 5,000, and a ton of paper may take 350,000 liters or only 60,000. Moreover, recycling the materials themselves can also greatly cut industrial water use and wastewater discharges. Manufacturing a ton of aluminum from scrap rather than virgin ore, for instance, can reduce the volume of water discharged by 97 percent.[75]

For the manufacturing industries that use a great deal of water—primary metals, chemicals, food products, pulp and paper, and petroleum—the cost of water is rarely more than 3 percent of total manufacturing expenses. Incentives to use water more efficiently

"Sweden's total water withdrawals in the mid-seventies were only half the level projected a decade earlier."

have come either from strict water allocations or stringent pollution control requirements. In Israel, where virtually all available fresh-water supplies are being tapped, the government has set quotas on the amount any industrial plant may receive. A water-use standard per unit of production is established for each industry, and a particular plant's allocation is then calculated by multiplying the standard by the anticipated level of production. As new technologies are developed, the standards are made more stringent. Consequently, average water use per unit value of industrial production has declined in Israel by 70 percent over the last two decades.[76]

In Sweden, industrial water use quintupled between 1930 and the mid-sixties but has since shown a marked decline. Strict environmental protection requirements for the pulp and paper industry, which accounts for about 80 percent of the country's industrial withdrawals, fostered widespread adoption of recycling technologies. Despite more than a doubling of production between the early sixties and late seventies, the industry cut its total water use by half—a fourfold increase in water efficiency. Indeed, largely because of these savings, Sweden's total water withdrawals in the mid-seventies were only half the level projected a decade earlier.[77]

Pollution controls spawned by federal and state laws are also helping to curb manufacturing water use in many areas of the United States. Surveys of California industries show, for example, that total water use in manufacturing declined during the seventies despite a 14 percent increase in the number of plants. Echoing Sweden's experience, the pulp and paper industry led in water reductions, with a 45 percent decline in withdrawals between 1970 and 1979. Nationwide, industrial withdrawals have not yet turned the corner, probably because of long delays in passing the pollution control requirements authorized by the Clean Water Act. Yet declines should occur when and where strict standards are enforced.[78]

Developing countries are in a prime position to take advantage of these new recycling technologies. Building water efficiency and pollution control into new plants is vastly cheaper than retrofitting old ones. Experience in the West shows that industries will have little incentive to adopt these measures without either sufficiently high water and wastewater fees or stringent pollution control requirements. Many of the technologies available are able to reduce water use and wastewater flows at least 90 percent and thus can contribute greatly to alleviating water supply and pollution problems in growing industrial areas. A recent study of an integrated iron and steel plant near São Paulo in Brazil, for example, showed that the plant was withdrawing 12,000 cubic meters of water per hour—highly polluted with the city's sewage—and that it was discharging 22,000 tons of iron oxide and 2,600 tons of grease annually into the nearby Santos estuary. For an estimated $15 million, or less than $1 per ton of annual production, the plant could install a recirculating water system that would cut water use by 94 percent and pollutant discharges by 99 percent.[79]

Household and other municipal water demands rarely account for more than 15 percent of a nation's water budget, and worldwide they claim only about 7 percent of total withdrawals. Yet storing, treating, and distributing this water, as well as collecting and treating the resulting wastewater, is increasingly costly. Large capital investments are required, making water and wastewater utilities especially sensitive to scarce capital and high interest rates. In the United States, for example, water and wastewater utilities require an average of $8.5 billion in new investment each year. Capital needs for 1982-90 are expected to total about $100 billion, and some estimates go much higher.[80] Reducing municipal water use can ease these financial burdens by allowing water and wastewater utilities to scale down the capacity of new plants, water mains, and sewer pipes and to cut the energy and chemical costs associated with pumping and treating the water.

Many household fixtures and appliances use much more water than necessary to perform their varied functions. Most toilets in the United States, for example, use 18-22 liters per flush, while water-conserving varieties recommended by the Plumbing Manufacturers Institute average about 13. A typical West German toilet requires only 9 liters per flush, and a new model that meets government standards uses about 7.5 liters, just a third as much as conventional U.S. models. Showerheads often spray forth 20 or more liters per minute; water-conserving designs can cut this at least in half. Water-efficient dish-

"In the United States, water and wastewater utilities require an average of $8.5 billion in new investment each year."

washers and washing machines can reduce water use 25-30 percent over conventional models. With simple conservation measures such as these, indoor water use can easily be reduced by a third.[81] (See Table 8.)

Consumers installing these devices and appliances will almost always save money, since they will reduce not only water use but the energy used in heating water. A typical household in the United States, for example, could expect investments in common water-saving fixtures and appliances to pay for themselves through lower water, sewer, and energy costs in just a few months, or within four years at most.[82] Israel, Italy, and the states of California, Florida, Michigan, and New York now have laws requiring the installation of various water-efficient appliances in new homes, apartments, and offices.[83]

Table 8: United States: Annual Household Water Use and Potential Savings With Simple Conservation Measures[1]

Activity	Share of Total Indoor Water Use	Without Conservation	With Conservation	Savings
	(percent)	(thousand liters per capita)		(percent)
Toilet flushing	38	34.5	16.4	52
Bathing	31	27.6	21.8	21
Laundry and Dishes	20	18.0	13.1	27
Drinking and Cooking	6	5.5	5.5	0
Brushing teeth, Misc.	5	4.1	3.7	10
Total	100	89.7	60.5	33

[1]Estimates based on water use patterns for a typical U.S. household. European toilets, for example, often use less water than the figures given here would imply.

Source: Adapted from U.S. Environmental Protection Agency, Office of Water Program Operations, *Flow Reduction: Methods, Analysis Procedures, Examples* (Washington, D.C.: 1981).

Despite its potential financial benefits to consumers and utilities, municipal conservation is still typically viewed only as a means of combating drought, rarely as a long-range water strategy. Programs developed by water-short communities to foster lasting reductions in water use, however, have yielded fruitful results. In Tucson, Arizona, a combination of price increases and public education efforts to encourage installation of household water-saving devices and replacement of watered lawns with desert landscaping led to a 24 percent drop in per capita water use. As a result, the Tucson utility's pumping costs were reduced and the drilling of new water-supply wells was deferred. Planners thus expected customer water bills to be lower over the long term than they would have been without the conservation efforts.[84]

In El Paso, Texas, one of the most water-short cities in the United States, pricing and education efforts are also credited with a substantial reduction in water use. Long-term water supply projections show conservation meeting about 15-17 percent of the city's future water needs. Besides slowing the rate of depletion of El Paso's underground water supplies, the conservation measures are saving water for an average cost of about $135 per 1,000 cubic meters—8 percent less than the average cost of existing water supplies.[85]

Many other options are available to reduce the demand for fresh water. Some areas are finding, for example, that brackish water and treated wastewater can meet many of their water needs. In Saudi Arabia, brackish water irrigates salt-tolerant crops such as sugar beets, barley, cotton, spinach, and date palms, thereby saving the best-quality water for drinking and other household uses. Treated municipal wastewater is also reused there to irrigate crops and gardens, to recharge aquifers, and as a supply for certain industries.[86] Power plants in Finland, Sweden, the United Kingdom, and the United States are beginning to use brackish water or saltwater for cooling.[87]

In perennially dry South Africa, water policy specifically calls upon users to "make use of the minimum quantity of water of the lowest acceptable quality for any process." Over the next several decades, cities and industries are projected to recycle between 60 and 70 per-

"People rarely pay the true cost of the water they use."

cent of the water they withdraw. Engineers estimate that the cost of treating raw sewage to a quality suitable for drinking is very likely competitive with that of developing the next surface water source.[88] In Israel, 30 percent of municipal wastewater was already being reused in 1981, most of it for irrigation. With completion of the Dan Region Wastewater Reuse Project serving the Tel Aviv metropolitan area, projections are that the proportion of municipal wastewater reused will climb to 80 percent by the turn of the century.[89]

Priorities for a New Water Economy

Much of the profligate waste and inefficiency in today's use of water results from policies that promote an antiquated illusion of abundance. People rarely pay the true cost of the water they use. Economists often suggest pricing water at its marginal cost—the cost of supplying the next increment from the best available source. Consumers would thus pay more as supplies become scarcer. Market forces would foster conservation and a reallocation of water supplies to their highest valued uses. In California, for example, the value added per cubic kilometer of water is 65 times greater in industry than in agriculture.[90] Increasing competition for water and rising prices thus dictate a shift in water use from farming to manufacturing. The extent to which a market-driven reallocation should take place is partially a political decision, since it would alter a region's basic character and social fabric; but by economic criteria, it is efficient.

In reality, water is rarely priced at marginal cost; charges often bear little relation to the real cost and quantity of water supplied. Many homeowners in the United Kingdom, for instance, are charged for water according to the value of their property, a practice that dates to Victorian times. In Indonesia, Malaysia, Saudi Arabia, South Africa, Tanzania, most East European countries, and many others, the government pays all or most of the capital costs for major irrigation projects.[91] Farmers in the United States supplied with irrigation water from federal projects pay, on average, less than a fifth of the real cost of supplying it.[92] Taxpayers are burdened with the remainder, and farmers use more water than they would if asked to pay its full cost.

When water users supply themselves rather than relying on a public project, they typically pay only the cost of getting the water to their farm, factory, or home. But if their withdrawals are diminishing a water source or harming an ecosystem, they should bear the costs that their private actions impose on society. American farmers pumping water from the Ogallala Aquifer, for example, pay nothing extra for the right to earn their profits by depleting an irreplaceable resource. On the contrary, many get a tax break by claiming a depletion allowance based on the drop in water level beneath their land that year. The greater the depletion, the greater the allowance—hardly an incentive to conserve.[93] A more appropriate policy would be to tax groundwater pumping in all areas where aquifers are being depleted. That way the public gets some compensation for the loss of its resource, and farmers are encouraged to curb their withdrawals.

In much of the Third World, where the cost per hectare of building new irrigation systems often exceeds per capita gross national product, pricing water at its full cost may not always be feasible. Water is often supplied for free or is heavily subsidized because it is so vital to food production. Yet most experts agree that the inefficient operation and poor maintenance of irrigation systems is largely due to farmers' perceptions that they have no responsibility for them. International lending agencies are now investing handsome sums to rehabilitate irrigation systems that sound operation and maintenance could have kept in good working order. Having farmers pay some share of water costs gives them a stake in the system, besides generating revenue to improve operations.[94]

A combined strategy of charging Third World farmers for some share of system costs and organizing them into "water user associations" to coordinate management tasks and the collection of fees appears a promising way of improving irrigation management. Arguing for more attention to pricing and water user organizations in Thailand, economist Ruangdej Srivardhana of Kasetsart University in Bangkok says that in order for Thai farmers to improve their practices "the feeling that the irrigation facilities belong to and are useful to them is crucial."[95] Charging a modest price for an initial allotment and higher fees for water used above this amount would encourage farmers to conserve without overburdening them. Moreover, where ground-

"Industries should pay the full cost of using water in their production."

water supplies are available, farmers may be able to profitably construct irrigation wells with minimal public support. In India, over 1.7 million private tubewells had been installed by the late seventies, aided by the availability of credit with very reasonable interest and repayment terms. For many farmers on the Indo-Gangetic Plain, installation of these wells has yielded rates of return greater than 50 percent.[96]

Water users must also begin to pay for treating the water they pollute. Especially in many areas of the Third World, water bodies cannot long be expected to provide a source of high-quality drinking and irrigation water *and* to dilute the increasing tonnage of waste dumped into them each year. Dilution alone simply cannot maintain adequate water quality in a society undergoing rapid industrialization and urbanization. Industries should pay the full cost of using water in their production, which includes the cost of discharging most of it in a form suitable for reuse. Controlling pollution is costly: Funds for protecting quality now account for over half the U.S. budget for water resource development and amount to $25 billion annually.[97] Developing countries may not have the financial resources to subsidize costly pollution controls while at the same time continuing to improve irrigation systems and install drinking water services. Industrialization should proceed in tandem with industries' ability to pay for controlling the pollution they generate. Sacrificing water quality for industrial growth cannot be a winning proposition in the long run.

Existing laws and methods for allocating water supplies are often heavily biased toward those wanting to withdraw water and against those desiring that it remain in place. The old English common law, which required that a riparian landowner not diminish the quantity or quality of water remaining for downstream users, inherently protected stream ecology and habitats. Yet this rule was changed early in the American experience to give riparians the right to "reasonable use" of the water, thus allowing for alterations in streamflows. In the drier states of the American West, an appropriative system was adopted that is even more biased toward withdrawals: Water rights are allocated successively to those who put water to "beneficial use." Establishing such a use, and thus a water right, often required an actual diversion from the stream. As legal expert James Huffman notes, this was not a problem "until the combination of changing values and diminishing water supplies brought the issue of instream flow maintenance to the public attention."[98]

A number of options exist for governments seeking to preserve an ecological balance in their rivers and streams. In the United States, for example, Montana passed a law in 1973 that allows government agencies to acquire prospective water rights. Much of the state's water has not yet been appropriated, so under this legislation a large share of it can be reserved to protect stream ecology. Because of these reserved rights, much of the Yellowstone River will never be withdrawn for use. Many rivers and streams in the United States, however, are already fully appropriated during the dry season of the year. Preserving water quality and fish and wildlife habitats thus requires some form of regulation that limits withdrawals during periods of diminished flow. One of the most powerful tools available, though as yet little used, is what legal experts call the "public trust" doctrine. Dating back to Roman times, it asserts that governments hold certain rights in trust for the public and can take action to protect them from private interests. Its application has potentially sweeping effects since even existing water permits or rights could be revoked in order to prevent violation of the public trust.[99]

In a landmark decision handed down in February 1983, the California Supreme Court declared that the water rights of the City of Los Angeles, which allow diversions from the Mono Lake Basin, are subject to the public trust doctrine. Mono Lake, a hauntingly beautiful water body on the eastern side of the Sierra, has diminished in surface area by a third, largely because Los Angeles is diverting water from its major tributaries. The lake is also becoming more saline, threatening its brine shrimp population, which in turn feeds millions of local and migratory birds. By invoking the public trust doctrine, the California Court paved the way for a state agency or the courts to decide that Los Angeles must reduce its diversions from the Mono Lake Basin. California law professor Harrison C. Dunning writes: "Although ramifications of the ruling may not be apparent for years, there can be no doubt that it will raise new obstacles for those who would divert California's natural stream flows to farm and city use. . . . From now on, the state must protect what the court calls 'the

"Planners and educators must dispel the myth that conservation is exclusively a short-term strategy to alleviate immediate crises."

people's common heritage of streams, lakes, marshlands and tidelands'."[100]

Where demands are already at the limits of the available supply, regulations may be necessary to put water use on a sustainable footing. Strategies geared toward balancing the water budget are lacking in most areas experiencing falling water tables or shrinking surface supplies. Despite pleas by hydrologists, for example, no Indian states have passed laws to regulate the installation of tubewells or to limit groundwater withdrawals. In the southern state of Tamil Nadu, authorities are doing little to curb overpumping that in some areas has caused groundwater levels to drop 30 meters in just a decade. Hydrologists note that the "long-term effects are probably understood, but until the water disappears, it is hardly likely that anyone is going to do anything about the situation."[101]

At least one example worth emulating has emerged in the United States: the 1980 Arizona Groundwater Management Act. Facing a rapidly dwindling water supply, the state is requiring its most overpumped areas to achieve "safe yield" by the year 2025. At this level no more groundwater is withdrawn than is recharged; the resource is thus in balance. Achieving this goal will by no means be painless. Conservation measures will be required of all water users and all groundwater withdrawals will be taxed. No subdivided land can be developed without proof of an assured water supply. If by the year 2006 it appears that conservation alone will not achieve the state's goal, the government can begin buying and retiring farmland. Shifts in Arizona's economy have already begun: Between 1978 and 1982, the state's irrigated area declined 8 percent. Other water-short regions should recognize that such shifts are bound to occur, and that they will be less traumatic if, as Arizona is doing, they are eased by thoughtful planning. Many governments will be watching as the real test of Arizona's law begins in the nineties.[102]

Finally, planners and educators must dispel the myth that conservation is exclusively a short-term strategy to alleviate droughts and other immediate crises. Only in such dry nations as South Africa and Israel is conservation made an integral part of planning future water supplies. In these countries, which are already tapping most of their available sources, continually striving to increase the efficiency of water use is imperative if growth is to continue. But even in nations with untapped rivers and aquifers, measures to conserve, recycle, and reuse fresh water may in many cases make the resource available at a lower cost and with less environmental disruption than developing new supplies. Conservation's potential will never be realized until it is analyzed as a viable long-term option comparable to drilling a new well or building a new reservoir.

Steps toward this end were taken in the United States during the late seventies. In a June 1978 water policy message to the nation, President Carter resolved to make conservation a national priority. Government agencies began to make federal grants and loans for water projects conditional upon inclusion of cost-effective conservation measures. Numerous analyses suggested that substantial savings would accrue both to the government and to communities and their residents from measures to curb water demand.[103] Unfortunately, the Reagan administration took several steps backward when it demoted these conservation requirements to voluntary guidelines and disbanded the Water Resources Council, which had been pushing for a more economically efficient and environmentally sound water policy. California has taken the lead where the federal government has faltered: A 1983 law requires every major urban water supplier in the state to submit by the end of 1985 a management plan that explicitly evaluates efficiency measures as an alternative to developing new supplies.[104]

Most governments continue to expect traditional dam and diversion projects to relieve regional water stresses. Yet the engineering complexities of these projects, along with their threats of ecological disruption, multibillion-dollar price tags, and 20-year lead times leave little hope that they will deliver water in time to avert projected shortages—if, indeed, they are completed at all. In the Third World, unless deforestation and erosion are curbed and irrigation systems are better managed and maintained, large projects may waste scarce capital and diminish the productivity of cropland. Moreover, even the most grandiose schemes will not be ultimate solutions to regional water problems. The Soviet Union's planned diversion of the Siberian rivers, for example, may meet only one-fourth of the deficit expected in Central Asia. Water delivered to Arizona through the Central Arizona Project will make up for only half of the state's annual groundwater depletions and thus will not alone balance the water budget. Against an insatiable demand, the best any dam or diversion can do is to slow the depletion of supplies or delay the day when they fall short.

In an era of growing competition for limited water sources, heightened environmental awareness, and scarce and costly capital, new water strategies are needed. Continuing to bank on new large water projects, and failing to take steps toward a water-efficient economy, is risky: Vital increases in food production may never materialize, industrial activity may stagnate, and the rationing of drinking-water supplies may become more commonplace.

Alternatives to large dam and diversion projects exist. Water crises need not occur. Securing more-dependable supplies in the Third World can and should continue, but it may better be done with smaller projects more amenable to coordinated land and water management, with incremental development of groundwater, and especially with joint management of surface and underground supplies. In water-short areas of industrial countries, people and economic activity must begin adapting to water's limited availability. Supplies in Soviet Central Asia, for example, simply cannot support a booming population and an expanding farming economy for long. Oasis cities such as Phoenix and Los Angeles can no longer expect to grow and thrive by draining the water supplies of other regions. Conservation and better management can free a large volume of water—and capital—for competing uses. Thus far, we have seen only hints of their potential.

Notes

1. Frits van der Leeden, *Water Resources of the World* (Port Washington, N.Y.: Water Information Center, Inc., 1975).

2. An annual supply of 1,000 cubic meters per person is typically given as necessary for a decent standard of living. See Carl Widstrand, ed., *Water Conflicts and Research Priorities* (Oxford, U.K.: Pergamon Press, 1980).

3. Vaclav Smil, *The Bad Earth: Environmental Degradation in China* (Armonk, N.Y.: M.E. Sharpe, Inc., 1984).

4. Malin Falkenmark and Gunnar Lindh, *Water for a Starving World* (Boulder Colo.: Westview Press, 1976); Gary S. Posz et al., "Water Resource Development in India," American Embassy, New Delhi, June 1980; food grain reduction from B.B. Sundaresan, "Water: A Vital Resource for the Developing World," in Peter G. Bourne, ed., *Water and Sanitation: Economic and Sociological Perspectives* (Orlando, Fla.: Academic Press, Inc., 1984).

5. Zaire River flow from Van der Leeden, *Water Resources of the World*; famine threat in Africa discussed in Lester R. Brown, "Securing Food Supplies," in Lester R. Brown et al., *State of the World 1984* (New York: W.W. Norton & Co., 1984).

6. Inquiry on Federal Water Policy, "Water is a Mainstream Issue: Participation Paper," Canadian Minister of Supply and Services, Ottawa, 1984; Mardjono Notodihardjo, "Indonesia's Water Resources," in W. Hall C. Maxwell, ed., *Water for Human Consumption*, Proceedings of the Fourth World Congress of the International Water Resources Association (Dublin: Tycooly International Publishing Ltd., 1983); United Nations Economic Commission for Europe (UNECE), *Long-Term Perspectives for Water Use and Supply in the ECE Region* (New York: United Nations, 1981).

7. William W. Kellogg and Robert Schware, "Society, Science and Climate Change," *Foreign Affairs*, Summer 1982.

8. USSR Committee for the International Hydrological Decade, *World Water Balance and Water Resources of the Earth* (Paris: UNESCO, 1974).

9. Rice yields with different degrees of water control from Asit K. Biswas, "Major Water Problems Facing the World," *International Journal of Water Resources Development*, April 1983.

10. Estimate of global irrigated area and its contribution to production from

W.R. Rangeley, "Irrigation—Current Trends and a Future Perspective," World Bank Seminar, Washington, D.C., February 15, 1983; irrigation demands based on FAO estimate for the 1974 World Food Conference that gross water demand for harvested crop irrigation averages 11,400 cubic meters per hectare. Estimate takes into account that rice requires twice as much water as wheat and other dry cereals. This figure, applied to an average expansion of 4 million irrigated hectares annually, led to estimate of an additional 820 billion cubic meters annually for irrigation by 2000.

11. Wayne B. Solley et al., *Estimated Use of Water in the United States in 1980* (Alexandria, Va.: U.S. Geological Survey, 1983).

12. See John Harte and Mohamed El-Gesseir, "Water and Energy," *Science*, February 10, 1978, and Norman L. Dalsted and John W. Green, "Water Requirements for Coal-Fired Power Plants," *Natural Resources Journal*, January 1984; percent consumed from Solley et al., *Estimated Use in the United States*.

13. Major water-using industries from United Nations, *Resource and Needs: Assessment of the World Water Situation*, prepared for the U.N. Water Conference, Mar del Plata, Argentina, March 1977; trends in European countries from UNECE, *Long-Term Perspectives for Water Use and Supply*; Swedish Preparatory Committee for the U.N. Water Conference, *Water in Sweden* (Stockholm: Ministry of Agriculture, 1977).

14. Development decade goals cited in Biswas, "Major Water Problems."

15. United Nations, *Resources and Needs*; Solley et al., *Estimated Use in the United States*.

16. UNECE, *Long-Term Perspectives for Water Use and Supply*; World Health Organization, *Drinking Water and Sanitation, 1981-1990* (Geneva: 1981).

17. Widstrand, *Water Conflicts and Research Priorities*.

18. Water rendered unusable by pollution by year 2000 estimated at 3,000 cubic kilometers in Robert P. Ambroggi, "Water," *Scientific American*, September 1980.

19. Zheng Guanglin, "Research Program on China 2000," Institute of Scientific and Technical Information of China, Beijing, draft, February 1984; Smil, *The Bad Earth*.

20. Smil, *The Bad Earth*.

21. U.N. Economic Commission on Latin America, *The Water Resources of Latin America: Regional Report*, Santiago, Chile, 1977; Bogota River cited in Peter Nares, "Colombian Towns Threatened by Polluted Bogota River," *World Environment Report*, May 30, 1984.

22. Thane Gustafson, "Transforming Soviet Agriculture: Brezhnev's Gamble on Land Improvement," *Public Policy*, Summer 1977.

23. Share of U.S. irrigated land from "Colorado High Plains Study: Summary Report," Resource Analysis Section, Colorado Department of Agriculture, Denver, Colo., November 1983; for background on the Ogallala's development, see Kenneth D. Frederick and James C. Hanson, *Water for Western Agriculture* (Washington, D.C.: Resources for the Future, 1982), and Morton W. Bittinger and Elizabeth B. Green, *You Never Miss the Water Till...* (Littleton, Colo.: Water Resources Publications, 1980).

24. Data on water depletion from U.S. Geological Survey, *National Water Summary 1983--Hydrologic Events and Issues* (Washington, D.C.: U.S. Government Printing Office, 1984).

25. U.S. Department of Agriculture, *Agricultural Statistics 1983* (Washington, D.C.: U.S. Government Printing Office, 1983) and Bureau of the Census, "1982 Census of Agriculture," U.S. Department of Commerce, Washington, D.C., 1984; Nebraska corn production statistics from U.S. Department of Agriculture, Economic Research Service, *Economic Indicators of the Farm Sector: Costs of Production 1982* (Washington, D.C.: U.S. Government Printing Office, 1983).

26. See Dean Abrahamson and Peter Ciborowski, "North American Agriculture and the Greenhouse Problem," Report of the Humphrey Institute Symposium on the Response of the North American Granary to Greenhouse Climate Change, Minneapolis, Minn., April 1983, and Kellogg and Schware, "Society, Science and Climate Change."

27. Tucson information from Tony Davis, "Trouble in a Thirsty City," *Technology Review*, August/September 1984; Texas and Mexico references in Tommy Knowles and Frank Rayner, "Depletion Allowance for Groundwater Mining: Pros and Cons," *Journal of the American Water Works Association*, March 1978.

28. Reference to Tamil Nadu in Widstrand, *Water Conflicts and Research Priorities;* China references from Smil, *The Bad Earth.*

29. Thomas G. Sanders, "Population Growth and Resource Management: Planning Mexico's Water Supply," *Common Ground,* October 1977; China references from "Sinking City Under Control," *Beijing Review,* February 23, 1981; Smil, *The Bad Earth;* Texas situation from Knowles and Rayner, "Depletion Allowance: Pros and Cons."

30. For U.S. citations, see U.S. Geological Survey, *National Water Summary 1983;* other countries cited in Tony Samstag, "Too Much of a Good Thing," *Development Forum,* April 1984.

31. Cropland figure from M.I. L'vovich and I.D. Tsigel'naya, "The Potential for Long-Term Regulation of Runoff in the Mountains of the Aral Sea Drainage Basin," *Soviet Geography,* October 1981; population and employment issues discussed in Thane Gustafson, "Technology Assessment, Soviet Style," *Science,* June 20, 1980.

32. Philip P. Micklin, Department of Geography, Western Michigan University, Kalamazoo, Mich., private communication, September 5, 1984; reference to scientists' projections from G.V. Voropayev et al., "The Problem of Redistribution of Water Resources in the Midlands Region of the USSR," *Soviet Geography,* December 1983.

33. Estimate of water level decline from O.K. Leont'yev, "Why Did the Forecasts of Water-Level Changes in the Caspian Sea Turn Out to be Wrong?," *Soviet Geography,* May 1984; background information from Grigorii Voropaev and Aleksei Kosarev, "The Fall and Rise of the Caspian Sea," *New Scientist,* April 8, 1982; Micklin, private communication; Caspian fisheries discussed in Philip P. Micklin, "International Environmental Implications of Soviet Development of the Volga River," *Human Ecology,* Vol. 5, No. 2, 1977.

34. Philip C. Metzger and Jennifer A. Haverkamp, "Instream Flow Protection: Adaptation to Intensifying Demands," The Conservation Foundation, Washington, D.C., June 1984.

35. Inquiry on Federal Water Policy, "Water is a Mainstream Issue."

36. Anupam Mishra, "An Irrigation Project That Has Reduced Farm Production," Centre for Science and Environment, New Delhi, 1981.

37. Global estimate from V.A. Kovda, "Loss of Productive Land due to Salinization," *Ambio*, Vol. 12, No. 2, 1983; India and Pakistan estimates from Gilbert Levine et al., "Water," prepared for Conference on Agricultural Production: Research and Development Strategies for the 1980's, Bonn, West Germany, October 8-12, 1979; other areas from Biswas, "Major Water Problems," and various other sources.

38. Estimate of reservoir capacity based on M.I. L'vovich, *World Water Resources and Their Future*, translation edited by Raymond L. Nace (Washington, D.C.: American Geophysical Union, 1979); figures on large dam construction from van der Leeden, *Water Resources of the World*, and from Philip Williams, "Damming the World," *Not Man Apart*, October 1983.

39. U.S. Geological Survey, *National Water Summary 1983*.

40. UNECE, *Long-Term Perspectives for Water Use and Supply*.

41. Williams, "Damming the World."

42. Donor agency inspections from U.S. General Accounting Office, *Irrigation Assistance to Developing Countries Should Require Stronger Commitments to Operation and Maintenance* (Washington, D.C.: U.S. General Accounting Office, 1983); John Madeley, "Big Dam Schemes—Value for Money or Non-Sustainable Development?," *Mazingira*, Vol. 7, No. 4, 1983.

43. For an excellent discussion of these water and land interactions, see Malin Falkenmark, "New Ecological Approach to the Water Cycle: Ticket to the Future," *Ambio*, Vol. 13, No. 3, 1984; Malaysia example from Eneas Salati and Peter B. Vose, "Amazon Basin: A System in Equilibrium," *Science*, July 13, 1984; Dominica example from Robert S. Goodwin, "Water Resources Development in Small Islands: Perspectives and Needs," *Natural Resources Forum*, January 1984.

44. For an assessment of selected large dams projects, see Environmental Policy Institute, "Fact Sheets on International Water Development Projects," Washington, D.C., 1984.

45. Asit K. Biswas, "Water Where It's Wanted," *Development Forum*, August/September 1983.

46. Yao Bangyi and Chen Qinglian, "South-North Water Transfer Project Plans," in Asit K. Biswas et al., eds., *Long-Distance Water Transfer* (Dublin: Tycooly International Publishing Ltd., 1983).

47. Bruce Stone, "The Chang Jiang Diversion Project: An Overview of Economic and Environmental Issues," in Biswas et al., *Long-Distance Water Transfer;* cost estimates also given in Asit K. Biswas, "US $12 Billion Plan to Redistribute China's Water Wealth," *South*, April 1982.

48. For discussion of Siberian diversion plans, see O.A. Kibal'chich and N.I. Koronkevich, "Some of the Results and Tasks of Geographic Investigations on the Water-Transfer Project," *Soviet Geography*, December 1983; quote is from Gustafson, "Technology Assessment, Soviet Style."

49. Philip P. Micklin, "Recent Developments in Large-Scale Water Transfers in the USSR," *Soviet Geography*, April 1984; Micklin, private communication, October 16, 1984.

50. Water-saving potentials and salinization risks from summary of remarks made by O.A. Kibal'chich at conference in Irkutsk, Soviet Union, August 1983, and published in *Soviet Geography*, December 1983.

51. U.S. Congressional Budget Office, *Efficient Investments in Water Resources: Issues and Options* (Washington, D.C.: U.S. Government Printing Office, 1983).

52. Thomas M. Power, "An Economic Analysis of the Central Arizona Project, U.S. Bureau of Reclamation," Economics Department, University of Montana, Missoula, Mont., 1978.

53. Costs to date from Steve Macauley, Supervisory Engineer for the State Water Project Analysis Office, California Department of Water Resources, private communication, October 23, 1984; pumping costs from California Department of Water Resources, *Management of the California State Water Project* (Sacramento: California Resources Agency, 1983).

54. Jack Foley, "Governor's Water Bill Dead for this Year," *San Jose Mercury News*, August 7, 1984; private communications with California Department of Water Resources personnel, June and August 1984.

55. Projects worldwide from Jay H. Lehr, "Artificial Ground-Water Recharge: A Solution to Many U.S. Water-Supply Problems," *Ground Water*, May/June 1982; Israel project cited in Robert P. Ambroggi, "Underground Reservoirs to Control the Water Cycle," *Scientific American*, May 1977.

56. California Department of Water Resources, *The California State Water Project--Current Activities and Future Management Plans* (Sacramento: California

Resources Agency, 1980); California Dept. of Water Resources, *Management of the Water Project;* Helen Peters, Groundwater Staff Specialist, California Department of Water Resources, private communication, October 1984; median cost estimate for new surface reservoirs from Ronald B. Robie, "Irrigation Development in California—Construction or Water Management?," in *Irrigation Challenges of the 80's* (St. Joseph, Mich.: American Society of Agricultural Engineers, 1981).

57. Environmental and Energy Study Institute, *Weekly Bulletin*, March 26, 1984; Russell Brown, Subcommittee on Water and Power, Senate Committee on Energy and Natural Resources, private communication, October 1984.

58. Widstrand, *Water Conflicts and Research Priorities.*

59. Smil, *The Bad Earth.*

60. Ambroggi, "Underground Reservoirs"; William R. Gasser, *Survey of Irrigation in Eight Asian Nations* (Washington, D.C.: U.S. Department of Agriculture, 1981); problems with the project cited in Ian Carruthers and Roy Stoner, *Economic Aspects and Policy Issues in Groundwater Development* (Washington, D.C.: The World Bank, 1981) and by Douglas Merrey, Agency for International Development, private communication, October 1984.

61. Wayne A. Pettyjohn, *Introduction to Artificial Ground Water Recharge* (Columbus, Ohio: National Water Well Association, 1981).

62. Lehr, "Artificial Ground-Water Recharge."

63. L'vovich, *World Water Resources and their Future.*

64. Office of Technology Assessment, *Water-Related Technologies for Sustainable Agriculture in U.S. Arid/Semiarid Lands* (Washington, D.C.: U.S. Government Printing Office, 1983); desalination cost estimates from U.S. Comptroller General, *Desalting Water Probably Will Not Solve the Nation's Water Problems, But Can Help* (Washington, D.C.: U.S. General Accounting Office, 1979); use in Arabian Peninsula from M.A. Khan et al., "Development of Supplies & Sanitation in Saudi Arabia," *African Technical Review*, June 1984.

65. A concise description of irrigation systems is contained in Office of Technology Assessment, *Water-Related Technologies for Sustainable Agriculture in U.S. Lands.*

66. Negev experiments from "Israel's Water Policy: A National Commitment," in Office of Technology Assessment, *Water-Related Technologies for Sustainable Agriculture in Arid/Semiarid Lands: Selected Foreign Experience* (Washington, D.C.: U.S. Government Printing Office, May 1983); Office of Technology Assessment, *Water-Related Technologies for Sustainable Agriculture in U.S. Lands*; Jay H. Lehr, "Increased Irrigation Efficiency Will Ultimately Silence the Water-Short Blues of the Wasteful West," *Ground Water*, March/April 1983.

67. *IDB News*, Inter-American Development Bank, Washington, D.C., Vol. 10, No. 4.

68. Efficiency ranges from J. Keller et al., "Evaluation of Irrigation Systems," in *Irrigation Challenges of the 80's*; tailwater reuse discussed in Gordon Sloggett, *Energy and U.S. Agriculture: Irrigation Pumping 1974-1980* (Washington, D.C.: U.S. Government Printing Office, 1982); E.G. Kruse et al., "Advances in Surface Irrigation," in *Irrigation Challenges of the 80's.*

69. Nebraska program from Paul E. Fischbach, "Irrigation Management (Scheduling) Application," in *Irrigation Challenges of the 80's*; California system described by Edward Craddock, California Department of Water Resources, Office of Water Conservation, private communication, June 21, 1984; California Department of Water Resources, "The Mobile Agricultural Water Conservation Laboratory," information pamphlet prepared by the Office of Water Conservation, Sacramento, Calif.

70. "Israel's Water Policy: A National Commitment."

71. U.S. General Accounting Office, *Irrigation Assistance to Developing Countries*; D.B. Kraatz, *Irrigation Canal Lining* (Rome: U.N. Food and Agriculture Organization, 1977).

72. Worth Fitzgerald, U.S. Agency for International Development, private communication, April 25, 1984.

73. Mark Svendsen et al., "Meeting the Challenge for Better Irrigation Management," *Horizons*, March 1983.

74. Harte and El-Gesseir, "Water and Energy"; "Thirsty Desert Plant Has Unique Water System," *The Phoenix Gazette*, June 27, 1984.

75. Ranges of water use for steel and paper from United Nations, *Resources and Needs*; reductions with aluminum recycling from R.C. Ziegler, "Environmental Impacts of Virgin and Recycled Steel and Aluminum," Calspan Corporation, Buffalo, N.Y., 1976.

76. Saul Arlosoroff, "Water Management Policies Under Scarce Conditions: A Case Study—Israel," presented at Conference on Water for the 21st Century: Will It Be There?, Dallas, Tex., April 1984.

77. Swedish Preparatory Committee, *Water in Sweden.*

78. Reductions by California pulp and paper industry from California Department of Water Resources, *Water Use By Manufacturing Industries in California, 1979* (Sacramento: California Resources Agency, 1982).

79. See 3M Company, "Low- or Non-Pollution Technology Through Pollution Prevention," prepared for United Nations Environment Programme, St. Paul, Minn., June 1982; Brazil study from Division for Industrial Studies, "Water Use and Treatment Practices and other Environmental Considerations in the Iron and Steel Industry," United Nations Industrial Development Organization, Vienna, Austria, December 1981.

80. John J. Boland, "Water/Wastewater Pricing and Financial Practices in the United States," Metametrics, Inc., Washington, D.C., August 1983.

81. For estimates of water and energy savings and costs of various water-conserving measures, see U.S. Environmental Protection Agency, Office of Water Program Operations, *Flow Reduction: Methods, Analysis Procedures, Examples* (Washington, D.C.: 1981); reference to West German toilets from *World Environment Report*, April 4, 1984.

82. U.S. Environmental Protection Agency, *Flow Reduction.*

83. Stefano Burchi, "Regulatory Approaches to the Use of Water for Domestic Purposes," *Natural Resources Forum*, July 1983; Barbara Yeaman, Consultant to Facilities Requirements Division, U.S. Environmental Protection Agency, private communication, August 10, 1984.

84. Adrian H. Griffin et al., "Changes in Water Rates and Water Consumption in Tucson, 1974 to 1978," *Hydrology and Water Resources in Arizona and the Southwest*, Vol. 10, 1979; Stephen E. Davis, "Tucson's Tools for Demand Management," *Hydrology and Water Resources in Arizona and the Southwest*, Vol. 8, 1979.

85. Lee Wilson and Associates, Inc., "Water Supply Alternatives for El Paso," prepared for El Paso Water Utilities Public Service Board, Santa Fe, N. Mex., November 1981.

86. M.A. Kahn et al., "Development of Supplies & Sanitation in Saudi Arabia.

87. Dennis J. Parker and Edmund C. Penning-Rowsell, *Water Planning in Britain* (London: George Allen & Unwin, 1980); Swedish Preparatory Committee, *Water in Sweden.*

88. Quote and estimates of advanced treatment costs from Axel F. Zunckel and Maria P. Oliveira, "South African Water Reuse Policy and its Practical Implications," in *Proceedings of the Water Reuse Symposium II, Vol. 1* (Denver, Colo.: AWWA Research Foundation, 1981); reuse projections from Mike Nicol, "South Africa Will Require Wastewater Recycling Before Year 2000, Experts Say," *World Environment Report*, June 27, 1984.

89. Hillel I. Shuval, "The Development of the Wastewater Reuse Program in Israel," in *Proceedings of the Water Reuse Symposium II.*

90. Value added figures cited in Ambroggi, "Water."

91. Great Britain practice from Burchi, "Regulatory Approaches to the Use of Water for Domestic Purposes"; subsidies in selected countries from J.A. Sagardoy et al., *Organization, Operation and Maintenance of Irrigation Schemes* (Rome: U.N. Food and Agriculture Organization, 1982).

92. U.S. Congressional Budget Office, *Efficient Investments in Water Resources* (Washington, D.C.: U.S. Government Printing Office, 1983).

93. Knowles and Rayner, "Depletion Allowance: Pros and Cons"; Institute of Agriculture and Natural Resources, Cooperative Extension Service, "IRS Extends Ground Water Depletion Deduction to Nebraska Irrigators," University of Nebraska, Lincoln, Neb., March 18, 1983.

94. Importance of improved operation and maintenance discussed by Guy Le Moigne, Irrigation Advisor, World Bank, private communication, April 20, 1984, and by Fitzgerald, private communication.

95. See Frances F. Korten, *Building National Capacity to Develop Water Users' Associations: Experience from the Philippines* (Washington, D.C.: The World Bank, 1982); quote from Ruangdej Srivardhana, "No Easy Management:

Irrigation Development in the Chao Phya Basin, Thailand," *Natural Resources Forum*, April 1984.

96. See James A. Seagraves and K. William Easter, "Pricing Irrigation Water in Developing Countries," *Water Resources Bulletin*, August 1983; B.D. Dhawan, *Development of Tubewell Irrigation in India* (New Delhi: Agricole Publishing Academy, 1983).

97. Peter Rogers, "Fresh Water," prepared for The Global Possible Conference, World Resources Institute, Wye, Md., May 2-5, 1984.

98. James Huffman, "Instream Water Use: Public and Private Alternatives," in Terry L. Anderson, ed., *Water Rights: Scarce Resource Allocation, Bureaucracy, and the Environment* (Cambridge, Mass.: Ballinger Publishing Company, 1983).

99. Ibid.; Metzger and Haverkamp, "Instream Flow Protection."

100. For an excellent review of this decision, see Ellen Sullivan Casey, "Water Law—Public Trust Doctrine," *Natural Resources Journal*, July 1984; Harrison C. Dunning, "A New Front in the Water Wars: Introducing the 'Public Trust' Factor," *California Journal*, May 1983.

101. Dhawan, *Development of Tubewell Irrigation in India*; Tamil Nadu observation from Widstrand, *Water Conflicts and Research Priorities*.

102. Arizona Groundwater Management Study Commission Staff, "Summary: Arizona Groundwater Management Act," briefing presented to the Arizona Groundwater Management Study Commission and the Arizona State Legislature, June 5, 1980; Scott Hanson and Floyd Marsh, "Arizona Ground-Water Reform: Innovations in State Water Policy," *Ground Water*, January/February 1982; decline in irrigated area from U.S. Department of Agriculture, *Agricultural Statistics 1983*, and U.S. Department of Commerce, "Census of Agriculture."

103. See Environmental Protection Agency, *Flow Reduction*, and Institute for Water Resources, *The Role of Water Conservation in Water Supply Planning* (Fort Belvoir, Va.: U.S. Army Corps of Engineers, 1970).

104. Policy changes under Reagan administration from "Water Resources," in The Conservation Foundation, *State of the Environment: An Assessment at Mid-Decade* (Washington, D.C.: 1984), and from Yeaman, private communication; California law from Reprint of Assembly Bill No. 797, *Legislative Council's Digest*, California Assembly, October 1983.

SANDRA POSTEL is a senior researcher with Worldwatch Institute and author of "Protecting Forests," in *State of the World 1984* (W. W. Norton, 1984). Prior to joining Worldwatch, she was a resource analyst with a California-based consulting firm where she researched water issues. She has studied geology and political science at Wittenberg University and resource economics and policy at Duke University.

THE WORLDWATCH PAPER SERIES

No. of Copies

______ 1. **The Other Energy Crisis: Firewood** by Erik Eckholm.
______ 2. **The Politics and Responsibility of the North American Breadbasket** by Lester R. Brown.
______ 3. **Women in Politics: A Global Review** by Kathleen Newland.
______ 4. **Energy: The Case for Conservation** by Denis Hayes.
______ 5. **Twenty-two Dimensions of the Population Problem** by Lester R. Brown, Patricia L. McGrath, and Bruce Stokes.
______ 6. **Nuclear Power: The Fifth Horseman** by Denis Hayes.
______ 7. **The Unfinished Assignment: Equal Education for Women** by Patricia L. McGrath.
______ 8. **World Population Trends: Signs of Hope, Signs of Stress** by Lester R. Brown.
______ 9. **The Two Faces of Malnutrition** by Erik Eckholm and Frank Record.
______ 10. **Health: The Family Planning Factor** by Erik Eckholm and Kathleen Newland.
______ 11. **Energy: The Solar Prospect** by Denis Hayes.
______ 12. **Filling The Family Planning Gap** by Bruce Stokes.
______ 13. **Spreading Deserts—The Hand of Man** by Erik Eckholm and Lester R. Brown.
______ 14. **Redefining National Security** by Lester R. Brown.
______ 15. **Energy for Development: Third World Options** by Denis Hayes.
______ 16. **Women and Population Growth: Choice Beyond Childbearing** by Kathleen Newland.
______ 17. **Local Responses to Global Problems: A Key to Meeting Basic Human Needs** by Bruce Stokes.
______ 18. **Cutting Tobacco's Toll** by Erik Eckholm.
______ 19. **The Solar Energy Timetable** by Denis Hayes.
______ 20. **The Global Economic Prospect: New Sources of Economic Stress** by Lester R. Brown.
______ 21. **Soft Technologies, Hard Choices** by Colin Norman.
______ 22. **Disappearing Species: The Social Challenge** by Erik Eckholm.
______ 23. **Repairs, Reuse, Recycling—First Steps Toward a Sustainable Society** by Denis Hayes.
______ 24. **The Worldwide Loss of Cropland** by Lester R. Brown.
______ 25. **Worker Participation—Productivity and the Quality of Work Life** by Bruce Stokes.
______ 26. **Planting for the Future: Forestry for Human Needs** by Erik Eckholm.
______ 27. **Pollution: The Neglected Dimensions** by Denis Hayes.
______ 28. **Global Employment and Economic Justice: The Policy Challenge** by Kathleen Newland.
______ 29. **Resource Trends and Population Policy: A Time for Reassessment** by Lester R. Brown.
______ 30. **The Dispossessed of the Earth: Land Reform and Sustainable Development** by Erik Eckholm.
______ 31. **Knowledge and Power: The Global Research and Development Budget** by Colin Norman.
______ 32. **The Future of the Automobile in an Oil-Short World** by Lester R. Brown, Christopher Flavin, and Colin Norman.
______ 33. **International Migration: The Search for Work** by Kathleen Newland.
______ 34. **Inflation: The Rising Cost of Living on a Small Planet** by Robert Fuller.
______ 35. **Food or Fuel: New Competition for the World's Cropland** by Lester R. Brown.
______ 36. **The Future of Synthetic Materials: The Petroleum Connection** by Christopher Flavin.
______ 37. **Women, Men, and The Division of Labor** by Kathleen Newland.

_____ 38. **City Limits: Emerging Constraints on Urban Growth** by Kathleen Newland.

_____ 39. **Microelectronics at Work: Productivity and Jobs in the World Economy** by Colin Norman.

_____ 40. **Energy and Architecture: The Solar and Conservation Potential** by Christopher Flavin.

_____ 41. **Men and Family Planning** by Bruce Stokes.

_____ 42. **Wood: An Ancient Fuel with a New Future** by Nigel Smith.

_____ 43. **Refugees: The New International Politics of Displacement** by Kathleen Newland.

_____ 44. **Rivers of Energy: The Hydropower Potential** by Daniel Deudney.

_____ 45. **Wind Power: A Turning Point** by Christopher Flavin.

_____ 46. **Global Housing Prospects: The Resource Constraints** by Bruce Stokes.

_____ 47. **Infant Mortality and the Health of Societies** by Kathleen Newland.

_____ 48. **Six Steps to a Sustainable Society** by Lester R. Brown and Pamela Shaw.

_____ 49. **Productivity: The New Economic Context** by Kathleen Newland.

_____ 50. **Space: The High Frontier in Perspective** by Daniel Deudney.

_____ 51. **U.S. and Soviet Agriculture: The Shifting Balance of Power** by Lester R. Brown.

_____ 52. **Electricity from Sunlight: The Future of Photovoltaics** by Christopher Flavin.

_____ 53. **Population Policies for a New Economic Era** by Lester R. Brown.

_____ 54. **Promoting Population Stabilization: Incentives for Small Families** by Judith Jacobsen

_____ 55. **Whole Earth Security: A Geopolitics of Peace** by Daniel Deudney

_____ 56. **Materials Recycling: The Virtue of Necessity** by William U. Chandler

_____ 57. **Nuclear Power: The Market Test** by Christopher Flavin

_____ 58. **Air Pollution, Acid Rain, and the Future of Forests** by Sandra Postel

_____ 59. **Improving World Health: A Least Cost Strategy** by William U. Chandler

_____ 60. **Soil Erosion: Quiet Crisis in the World Economy** by Lester Brown and Edward Wolf.

_____ 61. **Electricity's Future: The Shift to Efficiency and Small-Scale Power** by Christopher Flavin

_____ 62. **Water: Rethinking Management in an Age of Scarcity** by Sandra Postel

_____ **Total Copies**

Single Copy—$4.00

Bulk Copies (any combination of titles)
2-5: $3.00 each 5-20: $2.00 each 21 or more: $1.00 each

Calendar Year Subscription (1984 subscription begins with Paper 58)
U.S. $25.00 _____

Make check payable to Worldwatch Institute
1776 Massachusetts Avenue NW, Washington, D.C. 20036 USA

Enclosed is my check for U.S. $ _____

____
name

____
address

____
city **state** **zip/country**